You Aren'

You Aren't What You Eat

Fed Up with Gastroculture

Steven Poole

Union Books

'But *somebody* has to call "bullshit" – regularly –
on those of us who cook or write about food or
talk about it.'

Anthony Bourdain, *Medium Raw*

'It is a hard matter, my fellow citizens, to argue
with the belly, since it has no ears.'

Marcus Porcius Cato (attrib.)

Contents

Prologue: The Food Rave

On a crisp autumn evening in a north London street, a rôtisserie trailer is parked outside a garden flat, green fairy lights blinking on and off, warm chickens perfuming the air. A thirtyish hipster wanders out to where I'm standing with a friend on the pavement and drawls his unimpressed judgement of what is going on inside. 'I think the arancinis are not quite spicy enough,' he informs us, with an eaten-it-all-before air. 'Could have more flavour, not really exotic.' Right now I haven't the faintest idea what 'arancinis' are (or that arancini, like panini, is already an Italian plural), but I nod knowingly while typing his thoughts into my phone, and my friend keeps him talking. 'I thought the Korean burger was quite good,' the hipster goes on, without much kimchi-fired enthusiasm, 'but I think a lot of people don't make their food with enough *shbang* . . . They kind of cater to the middle of the road.' Twenty-five years ago, he could have been an indie-rock fan bemoaning the blandness of chart music. Now

I

he's a social-smoking, foodier-than-thou critic at a 'Food Rave'.

I found the Food Rave advertised online and knew I had to attend. I met my friend in a nearby pub first, and we spent a couple of pints of bitter debating whether we should have brought glowsticks, or if we would bump into the Happy Mondays dancer-cum-mascot Bez, waving giant chicken drumsticks in place of his habitual maracas, warm poultry juice glistening on his chin as he stared into the middle distance, jerking his body to an unheard soundtrack of gustatory trance.

The name of the Food Rave, as I will gradually realize over the course of writing this book, is entirely appropriate for a modern culture in which food is the last ingestible substance you can indulge in with fanatical obsessiveness without being frowned upon by society. Alex James, the Blur bassist turned gentleman cheese farmer and *Sun* food columnist, has said: 'My 20th birthday party was all about booze, my 30th birthday was about drugs, and now I realise that my 40s are about food.'[1] And he is not alone. Food replaces drugs in the gently ageing food-fancier's pantheon of pleasure, and brings along with it traces of the old pharmaceutical vocabulary. You hear talk of taking a 'hit' of a dish or its sauce, as though from a spliff or bong; and a food-obsessive in hunter-gatherer mode is thrilled to 'score' a few chanterelle mushrooms, as though he has had to buy them from a dodgy-looking gent on a murky Camden street corner. (Cheeky Jamie Oliver, part of whose charm lies in his air of dubious legality, mines this seam concertedly, ducking into a pie shop 'to score a taste of the old school'.)[2] Food is valued for its psychotropic 'rush'; Nigella Lawson refers to salted caramel as 'this Class A foodstuff'.[3] Yes, food is the new drugs for former Britpoppers and the Ecstasy generation, a safer and more respectable hedonic tool, the key to a comfortingly domesticized high.

Arriving at the Food Rave and feeling a little peckish, we squeeze through the front door, down the hall, and into the garden, which is crammed with British food producers affably selling their wares to 150 or so youngish and hungry customers. People are ambling slowly through the throng alongside tented stalls that house people cooking and selling venison burgers, 'Mauritian Street Food', Italian sausages, and those Korean burgers: according to their Scottish explicator, who talks while her colleague cooks, their special ingredient, the spiced cabbagey condiment kimchi, is 'one of the top five health foods in the world'.

There are also 'raclett [*sic*] sandwiches', which customers are invited to 'punk up' with extra pickles; a serious knot of people studiously tasting different olive oils on bits of torn bread; a tent housing 'artisan' chocolate bars (for a slab roughly five by eight centimetres, or what I would call half a bar of chocolate, they want four quid); a married couple who, sweetly, have just tried oysters for the first time together (she liked them; he didn't); and, thankfully, a cheerful chap serving excellent draught ale. Inside, there are breadmaking and other culinary 'demonstrations' in the kitchen; puddings and cakes in the living room; and musicians playing tasteful acoustic folk on a wrought-iron balcony. The raviest character on the whole scene is a man with a head-mounted torch sharpening his knife over an enormous salmon fillet laid sacrificially on a plank.

Despite the connotations of illegal excitement that the name Food Rave deliberately plays on, there is little that is 'underground' about this quite pleasant event: the host has no doubt acquired the proper licences for the serving of liquor, and a man is wandering around filming the gobbling crowd with a television-grade video camera. It's much like a miniature, nocturnal version of any good street food market, and in a way is disappointing for its lack of displays of extreme eating or utterly repulsive contraband dishes featuring diced dog or craniotomized monkey, which might have given proceedings an edge of forbidden pleasure.

There is one corner of weirdness, in the shape of a colourfully wrapped woman sitting at a tiny table in the hall offering Tarot readings. I notice her only when attempting to rest my ale on the tiny table, something the cards violently forbid, at least in her interpretation. By coincidence, when we are outside on the street later, the hipster-critic tells us that his girlfriend is inside having a reading. 'It's quite funny that she's having her Tarot read because I read Tarot cards,' he says, with the kind of studied casualness one might use to announce that one can levitate. There is a moment of reverent

4

silence, and then my friend leaps to the rescue. How come, he asks. 'Because I can, I've got a talent for it,' the hipster says airily. 'It makes no sense to me, I'm not a scientist.' The idea that, if anyone in the vicinity were a scientist, they would be able to make sense of his ability to read Tarot cards is almost charming in its innocence. Granted, this is a diluted and spiceless version of the dark arts, glibly appropriated by the New Age reflex of the modern hipster, and yet it still seems odd, the irruption into a miniature eating festival of the occult. But this, it will become clear to me, is just another instance of the general rule that, the more obsessed people become by food, the more they are likely to believe in all other kinds of woo-woo bullshit.

By the time the hipster has progressed to telling us that he and his girlfriend have been 'trying to do that cooking of a whole lamb with the hay', but that the hay caught fire and reduced the whole animal to ash, I am losing the will to live. Eventually we manage to plunge back into the garden, at the end of which a friendly mixologist is disbursing the most delicious cocktails. Rave on.

I.

You Aren't What You Eat

Western industrial civilization is eating itself stupid. We are living in the Age of Food. Cookery programmes bloat the television schedules, cookbooks strain the bookshop tables, celebrity chefs hawk their own brands of weird mince pies (Heston Blumenthal) or bronze-moulded pasta (Jamie Oliver) in the supermarkets, and cooks in super-expensive restaurants from Chicago to Copenhagen are the subject of hagiographic profiles in serious magazines and newspapers. Food festivals (or, if you will, 'Feastivals') are the new rock festivals, featuring thrilling live stage performances of, er, cooking. As one dumbfounded witness of a stage appearance by Jamie Oliver observed: 'The girls at the front – it's an overwhelmingly female crowd – are already holding up their iPhones [. . .] A group in front of me are saying, "Ohmigodohmigodohmigod" on a loop [. . .] "I love you, Jamie," yells a girl on the brink of fainting.'[1]

If you can't watch cooking on television or in front of your face, you can at least read about it. Vast swathes of the internet have been taken over by food bloggers who post photographs of what they have eaten from an edgy street stall or at an aspirational restaurant, and compose endlessly scrollable pseudoerotic paeans to its stimulating effects. According to the spring 2011 Bookscan data, British sales of books in nearly all literary genres were down, except for the categories of 'food and drink' (up 26.2 per cent), followed by 'religion' (up 13 per cent). (Before 1990, the bibliographic category of 'food and drink' didn't even exist.)[2] That food and religion alone should buck the negative trend is no coincidence, for modern food books are there to answer metaphysical or 'lifestyle' rather than culinary aspirations, and celebrity chefs themselves are the gurus of the age. The literary and visual rhetoric of food in our culture has become decoupled from any reasonable concern for nutrition or environment: it has become, instead, an ersatz spiritualism. We no longer trust our politicians or our priests; we now expect our cooks to fulfil both roles.

No surprise, then, that so many people successful in other fields now want to become famous in food. Models (Sophie Dahl, Lorraine Pascale) and actors (Gwyneth Paltrow) write cookbooks and food blogs; Francis Ford Coppola and Jon Bon Jovi open restaurants. When everyone is crazy about food, a cook – the ultimate food authority – is the thing to be. It's not unlucrative, either: the American queen of TV food, Rachael Ray, pulls in an estimated $18 million a year.[3]

Occasionally a cook's desire for panmedia world domination can overreach – in summer 2011, the food-based romcom *Love's Kitchen*, starring Gordon Ramsay, grossed a possibly disappointing total of £121 over its UK launch weekend: roughly the price of food for one at Restaurant Gordon Ramsay in London.[4] But with supermarket promotions, chains of branded restaurants, literary overproduction and everything else, the modern chef can certainly put food on his own plate. There is now something called a Jamie At Home party, our age's equivalent of the Tupperware party. For a Jamie At Home party, Jamie Oliver does not actually come to your home. Instead, a friend (or more likely an acquaintance of a friend, as I heard it from one horrified attendee of such a 'party') comes round and tries to sell everyone some Jamie Oliver-branded cookware.

It is not in our day considered a sign of serious emotional derangement to announce publicly that 'chocolate mousse remains the thing I feel most strongly about',[5] or to boast that dining with celebrities on the last night of Ferran Adrià's restaurant El Bulli, in Spain, 'made me cry'.[6] It is, rather, the mark of a Yahoo not to be able and ready at any social gathering to converse in excruciating detail and at interminable length about food. Food is not only a safe 'passion' (in the tellingly etiolated modern sense of 'passion' that just means liking something a lot); it has become an obligatory one. The unexamined meal, as a pair of pioneer modern 'foodies' wrote in the 1980s, is not worth eating.[7] Most cannily, the department

8

of philosophy at the University of North Texas announced in 2011 its 'Philosophy of Food Project', no doubt having noticed which way the wind was blowing, and presumably hoping that it would be able to trick food-obsessives into hard thinking about other topics.[8] One can of course think philosophically about food, as about anything at all, but that is not what is going on in our mainstream gastroculture.

Where will it all end? Is there any communication or entertainment or social format that has not yet been commandeered by the ravenous gastrimarge for his own gluttonous purpose? Does our cultural 'food madness', as the *New York Times* columnist Frank Bruni suggests, tip into 'food psychosis'?[9] Might it not, after all, be a good idea to worry more about what we put into our minds than what we put into our mouths?

People with an overweening interest in food have been calling themselves 'foodies' since a *Harper's & Queen* article entitled 'Cuisine Poseur' in 1982, one of whose editors then co-wrote the semi-satirical *Official Foodie Handbook* of 1984.[10] The *OED*'s very first citation of 'foodie' is from 1980, an oozing *New York* magazine celebration of the mistress of a Parisian restaurant and her 'devotees, serious foodies'.[11] 'Foodie' has now pretty much everywhere replaced 'gourmet', perhaps because the latter more strongly evokes privilege and a snobbish claim to uncommon sensory discrimination – even though those qualities are rampant among the 'foodies' themselves. The word 'foodie', it is true, lays claim to a kind of cloying, infantile cuteness which is in a way appropriate to its subject; but one should not allow them the rhetorical claim of harmless innocence implied. The *Official Foodie Handbook* spoke of the 'foodism' worldview; I propose to call its adherents foodists.

The term 'foodist' is actually much older, used from the late nineteenth century for hucksters selling fad diets (which is quite apt, as we shall see); and as late as 1987 one *New York Times* writer proposed it semi-seriously as a positive description, to replace the unlovely 'gastronaut': 'In the tradition of nudist, philanthropist and Buddhist, may I suggest "foodist", one who is enthusiastic about good eating?'[12] The writer's joking offer of 'nudist' as an analogy is telling. I like 'foodist' precisely for its taint of an -ism. Like a racist or a sexist, a foodist operates under the prejudices of a governing ideology, viewing the whole world through the grease-smeared lenses of a militant eater.

Foodism is not itself an eating disorder but a disorder of culture; though the two perhaps cannot be completely separated. There are of course serious illnesses related to eating (anorexia, bulimia). But one proposed new disorder waiting in the wings has an intriguing relationship with our mass cultural foodism: it is called 'orthorexia'. From the Greek *orthos* (straight or correct), orthorexia means an obsession with eating correctly, according to some understanding of what the healthiest diet is. It was coined by a cook and organic farmer turned 'alternative physician', Steven Bratman, who began to have doubts about 'nutritional medicine' and its 'chaotic' recommendations.[13]

One of our most enthusiastic hawkers of nutritionism is the quondam 'Doctor' Gillian McKeith, of *You Are What You Eat* book and TV show fame. (Known to my Aunt Rose and others as 'the poo doctor', McKeith was persuaded to stop advertising herself as a doctor in 2007, once it was revealed that her 'PhD' came by 'distance learning' from the academically unaccredited American Holistic College of Nutrition. You don't need any medical qualifications to call yourself a 'nutritionist', as you do to be a dietitian.)[14] McKeith's 2008 *Food Bible* contains weird lifestyle recommendations that could fill one's days. 'Get into the habit of skin brushing,' she burbles, as one means of 'detox'.[15] She promises: 'We have the power to excel forward to new advanced levels and heights of excellent [*sic*] if we take up the reins', and informs us helpfully as to what we should scoff (garlic, berries, broccoli, 'liquid algae') in order to cure various illnesses.[16] Do you perhaps have an 'anxiety disorder'? That will be a 'magnesium deficiency'.[17] People suffering from backache should avoid aubergines since 'they may promote congestion in the kidneys'.[18]

The doctor and *Bad Science* author Ben Goldacre has observed that nutritionists can't satisfy themselves with the healthy-eating advice that everyone already knows. (As the American author of *The Omnivore's Dilemma*, Michael Pollan, boils it down: 'Eat food. Not too much. Mostly plants.')[19] Indeed, it might seem sensible for a professional nutritionist constantly to expand the range of advice on offer, just as celebrity cooks have constantly to invent novel recipes in order to sell their latest literary work. Meanwhile, Gillian McKeith is here to tell us that 'liver stagnation' may be a cause of depression – as might 'food sensitivities'.[20]

Ah, food sensitivities. McKeith is a great proponent of the idea that food sensitivities or 'intolerances' are the root cause of innumerable modern ills. According to her, they are 'a 21st-century epidemic', though why they should have become so in recent years is a mystery, if it is not thanks to people like McKeith herself blaming them for everything that could possibly go wrong in your life.[21] In her caring desire to help those with even the most serious illnesses, McKeith does not shrink from promoting her wares to people with AIDS, for whom her sensitive advice includes the following: 'It is probably worthwhile getting tested for food intolerances if you are not sure which foods affect you. See www.gillianmckeith.info for a home food-intolerance testing kit.'[22] Surely only a cynic would suggest that McKeith has a vested interest in talking up the prevalence of food 'intolerances' because she is selling a 'kit' through her website.

There are some well-established food intolerances, such as those relating to lactose and gluten, though the proportion of people with coeliac disease (one in 133 people and rising, though no one knows why) might not fully explain the increasing popularity of a wheat-averse diet or 'gluten-free' foodstuffs, named as though gluten were a disgusting additive, and often now so labelled even when they never contained any gluten in the first place.[23] Dull facts about wheat and milk alone, in any case, won't keep a 'nutritionist' in business, so 'intolerances' have multiplied among the faddists to a vast constellation of possible irritants: McKeith's home-testing intolerance kit 'tests for 113 foods' including apples, parsley, vanilla, chicken, and hops. (McKeith is very down on alcohol and coffee.) Such kits (based on 'IgG antibody tests') were the subject of investigation by a 2007 House of Lords commission, which in its report referred to an 'absence of stringent scientific evidence' for their effectiveness. One medical expert, Consultant Allergist Dr Glenis Scadding, told the Lords that IgG tests for food allergy were a waste of money, and 'liable to leave patients on diets that are inadequate'.[24]

McKeith speaks not only of 'intolerances' but also 'sensitivities' and 'allergies', while claiming that just about anything that ails you can be attributed to one. She encourages people to stump up for her testing kit if they 'regularly experience any of the following symptoms', including 'Anxiety, Fatigue, Itching, Headaches, Nausea, and Tiredness'. I confess that I experienced all those at once after reading *Gillian McKeith's Food Bible*.

Food 'intolerances' are the flipside of positive foodism: just as food is the source of all pleasure for 'foodies', for the 'intolerant' all psychic problems can be traced to food and fixed by fiddling with it. It is understandable why that should be a comforting thought: it is a kind of physiological Stoicism, according to which you are entirely in control of your reactions to an inhospitable world. Nutritionism is thus the modern pseudoscientific equivalent of the ancient doctors' dubious theories about foodstuffs, surveyed in *The Anatomy of Melancholy* by Robert Burton as he tried to establish what kind of meals would be most helpful to the depressive. ('Of roots, parsnips and potatoes are highly approved; but onions, garlick, scallions, carrots, and raddishes, are flatulent, and dangerous.')[25] The French philosopher Michel Foucault argued in a 1983 television interview that, in modern times, sex had replaced the ancients' focus on diet as a means of defining oneself.[26] But three decades on, food is undeniably back on top.

Very possibly, eating more of some things and less of others might improve one's wellbeing (beyond the immediate pleasure of satiety), but the functionalist, medicinal attitude to food is liable to induce an unrealistic confidence in one's ability to control fate. As a foodist and 'nutritional therapist' told the *Guardian*: 'There are lots of things in this world we can't control. I find it really empowering that I can control my health and the way I feel through what I eat.'[27] As McKeith promises, too: 'Your health really is in your hands, and your kitchen.'[28] If it's tempting just to read this as harmless reassuring nonsense, consider the flipside: if you get sick, it

14

must be your fault. (As it is for the devotees of 'Christian Science', according to whom disease and disability are the wages of sin.) Ben Goldacre, for one, diagnoses nutritionism as 'a manifesto of right-wing individualism. You are what you eat, and people die young because they deserve it. *They* choose death, through ignorance and laziness, but *you* choose life, fresh fish, olive oil, and that's why you're healthy.'[29]

Another celebrated modern 'nutritionist', Patrick Holford, conveys a similar message in his millions-selling *Optimum Nutrition Bible*: you can choose to be healthy through eating the proper foods, and if you get sick it's your funeral. ('Most disease,' he declares, is 'the result of sub-optimum nutrition.')[30] As with McKeith, the effect of Holford's approach may be to worry the reader into health-paranoia by describing perfectly normal experiences as 'symptoms' of bad nutrition. Do you find it 'hard to get up in the morning' or have bouts of 'anger' or 'apathy'? Then what do you know, 'you may have an adrenal hormonal imbalance'. And naturally, 'this warrants investigation by a nutritionist'.[31] Meanwhile, we learn that 'many of the twentieth century's most common diseases are associated with a shortage of antioxidant nutrients, and helped by their supplementation' – which is a pleasingly fortunate medico-commercial synergy, since Holford also sells antioxidant pills himself.[32]

Some of Holford's advice is perfectly sensible: eat more whole grains and less refined sugar. But an entrepreneurial nutritionist can't leave it at that. So seven years after the

Optimum Nutrition Bible, there appeared *Patrick Holford's New Optimum Nutrition Bible*, in which he adds to his compendium of creative theories the advice to 'Eat Right for Your Blood Type' (following 'the pioneering research of naturopath Peter D'Adamo'), plus the opinions that vitamin C might be better at treating AIDS than the antiretroviral drug AZT, and that 'possible culprits' for autism 'include diet, vaccinations and digestive disorders',[33] as well as more inspirational hints that cancer could be combated by correct eating.[34]

Lest this seem a mean-spirited attack on a food guru who has helped, at least in his own estimation, countless people whose 'lives have literally been transformed',[35] I will leave the last word to Holford himself. Responding woundedly to a demolition job on him by Ben Goldacre in 2007, Holford protested that he didn't just award himself his own 'nutritionist' qualifications. Heaven forbid. As Holford explained: 'For the record, I did not confer my own diploma, as he states. The board of the Institute for Optimum Nutrition (ION), which is an educational trust that I founded in 1984, awarded me an honorary diploma.'[36] An inspiring example to us all.

If orthorexia is a real phenomenon and on the rise, it can hardly be denied that the modern proponents of nutritionism like Patrick Holford and Gillian McKeith bear a lot of the responsibility. But it is tempting to go even further, and to say that our modern mania for television cooking shows, celebrity chefs, recipe books, food festivals, food gadgets, and the like is a generalized orthorexia writ large all over our distended cultural stomach. Remove orthorexia's concern with 'health' in a medical sense, and the similarities with mainstream foodism are striking. In 2004, an Italian team of researchers laid out some potential diagnostic criteria for 'orthorexia nervosa'. The orthorexic, they wrote, displays a 'search for an identity and spirituality in eating behaviour', just as foodists do. 'The orthorexic sufferer spends a great deal of his time thinking about food', just as foodists do. The orthorexic's eating behaviour 'generates a feeling of superiority over the lifestyle and eating habits of other people', just as that of foodists does.[37]

The orthorexic and the foodist are united in the moronic Lego-block materialism that says you are what you eat. For a generation that has nothing external left to believe in, the body is the last appropriate object of worship. Your body is a temple, and you become extremely interested in what goes into it (as well as, like McKeith, what comes out). The external world is reduced to possible bodily inputs.

The amiably complacent old gourmand Jean Anthelme Brillat-Savarin, a French lawyer and politician active around the turn of the nineteenth century and the author of *The Physiology of Taste* – a compendium of cooking instructions, anecdotes of Dinners What I Have Ate, and theorized ingluviosity – is still cited with reverence by modern foodists because he brings a patina of literary sophistication and respectability to their fixation. Perhaps most famous among his dicta is: 'Tell me what you eat: I will tell you what you are.'[38] Well, I for one am not part roast chicken and part crisps. The promise is obviously preposterous, as though one could deduce the philosophy of Wittgenstein from a close analysis of his breakfasts; but it does sanction the use of food as a marker of class distinction and aesthetic sensitivity by those wealthy enough so to use it: 'only the man of intellect,' burbles Brillat-Savarin, 'knows how to eat'.[39] (Brillat-Savarin himself was, like Gillian McKeith, also a hater of coffee, making him rather uncongenial to my mind, though his manner of expressing it recalls charmingly a more innocent age of grape-worship: 'A man of sound constitution can drink two bottles of wine a day, and live to a great age; the same man could not stand a like quantity of coffee for the same period; he would go out of his mind or die of consumption.')[40]

Like Brillat-Savarin, the witty modern foodist Jay Rayner also portrays foodism as refined and judicious labour: 'Real enthusiasm around food is not indiscriminate,' he insists. 'It's not about the lowest common denominator [. . .] It takes hard work. It takes effort.' He pities non-foodists, or those who have a 'stunted interest in their dinner', for supposing that foodism is 'about a lack of control, when it's exactly the opposite. It's about taking control: of appetites, of possibilities, of yourself.'[41] So expressed, foodism can be seen again to share the desire for perfect self-mastery that is characteristic of orthorexia, as well as a further will to dominion over external 'possibilities'. Rayner's foodist micromanifesto is thus also nicely in tune with Roland Barthes's aperçu that the advertising rhetoric of the emerging 'nutritional consciousness' in the 1960s, which promised 'energy' and 'alertness', was not about wisdom or asceticism; it was about power. 'The energy furnished by a consciously worked-out diet is mythically directed, it seems, toward an adaptation of man to the modern world,' Barthes observed.[42]

It might reasonably be supposed at this point that one so down on foodists as I am must be some kind of morose food-hater or puritan anti-sensualist in general. But I like food, not just because it keeps me alive, and I eat a fair bit of it. I ate a lot of very nice food in particular during five years I spent living in Paris, which has made me especially hard to please in matters of pâté, bread, parmentier de confit de canard, and chocolate. I stand shoulder to shoulder with the great muncher of pork, Charles Lamb, when he admits, in his 1821 essay 'Grace Before Meat': 'I am no Quaker at my food. I confess I am not indifferent to the kinds of it.'[43] Like many people, and all foodists, I would rather eat good food than crap. But I don't ordinarily spend much time actually thinking about it; and before I decided to write this book I had never felt an inclination to watch television food shows or read cookbooks or exotic accounts of foodist voyages. One can enjoy food for what it is (food) while still feeling that such a devotion to food in the general culture represents a kind of perversity or decadence, an inward-turning dissipation of psychic and intellectual resources.

My point is not primarily that we, the globally wealthy, daydream about elaborate food while millions starve (severe famines, in the analysis of the economist Amartya Sen, are usually the result not of food shortages per se, but of inadequate distribution).[44] Nor even that the foodism of the wealthy can seem obscene in the context of their own societies: at the time of this writing, 15 per cent of the US population relies on food stamps to be able to eat enough.[45] (Jon Bon Jovi's restaurant venture, to his great credit, is a 'pay-what-you-can' restaurant in New Jersey called the Jon Bon Jovi Soul Kitchen.)[46] Nor, again, that it might seem strange, in the context of such increasing deprivation and 'food insecurity', that there should still exist a branch of food science devoted to 'diet' products, ministering to what one researcher has called the commercial 'need to develop foods that are low in calories'.[47]

All these things might count as charges against the louring foodist weather that hangs over us all; but one can as reasonably wish to concentrate on the harm that media foodism does to the culture itself. Philosophical idealism, said Theodor Adorno, is 'the belly turned mind', and 'rage' is its hallmark.[48] Foodism is the rage of the belly without any consequent sublimation into mind. In 1985, the novelist Angela Carter read the *Official Foodie Handbook* for the *London Review of Books* and complained that the age, even then, was one of 'piggery triumphant'. (She noted with horror that there were now food pages in the *Guardian*, of all places.)[49]

Heaven knows what she would say now. We are crowded and harangued by people of evident thoughtfulness who are infatuated with food when they could be doing so much else with their time and creative energy, were they not alternately salivating like excited dogs and sluggard-brained with the viscous blood flow of over-challenged digestion.

2.

Soul Food

The Jon Bon Jovi Soul Kitchen is aptly named. Everywhere in the ideology of foodism we see a yearning for food to be able to fill a spiritual void. Food is about 'spirituality' and 'expressing our identity', claims modern food-knight Michael Pollan.[1] His celebrated catechism of modern foodism, *The Omnivore's Dilemma*, speaks of eating with a 'full consciousness', and claims that every meal has its 'karmic price'; it ends with the declaration that 'what we're eating is never anything more or less than the body of the world'.[2] And so chewing on pork products becomes a sublime union of self with planet, a Gaian eucharist.

Note, too, how many manuals of eating are termed 'bibles': apart from Holford's *Optimum Nutrition Bible* and McKeith's *Food Bible*, there is also a *Baby Food Bible*, a *Whole Food Bible*, a *Gluten-Free Bible*, a *Party Food Bible*, a *Spicy Food Lover's Bible*, and so on ad nauseam or perhaps ad astra. If you don't want the Judeo-Christian overtones that come with biblical foodism, you can instead attain communion with the druids, a possibility noted by Hugh Fearnley-Whittingstall in the late 1990s: 'I suspect the fact that wild mushrooms (and the pursuit of them) have become popular alongside the burgeoning interest in New Age spiritualism may not be entirely coincidental.'[3]

Food, then, is considered the appropriate sustenance for all kinds of spiritual snackishness. But to suppose that eating can nourish the spirit looks like a category mistake: just the sort of category mistake that led the early church to define 'gluttony' as a sin. (Man does not live by bread alone.) Gluttony, on the original understanding, wasn't necessarily a matter of eating too much; it was the problem of being excessively interested in food, whatever one's actual intake of it. Gluttony was, as Francine Prose (author of a pert monograph, *Gluttony*) puts it, all about the 'inordinate desire' for food, which makes us 'depart from the path of reason'.[4] (That diagnoses the figure of 'loathsome Gluttony' in Spenser's *The Faerie Queene*, 'Whose mind in meat and drinke was drowned so'.)[5] And the theologian Thomas Aquinas agreed with Pope Gregory that gluttony can be committed in five different ways, among which are seeking more 'sumptuous foods' or wanting foods that are 'prepared more meticulously'.[6] In this sense (whether we agree with it or not), all modern foodists, as the *Atlantic* writer B.R. Myers argues in his incisive 'Moral Crusade Against Foodies', are certainly gluttons.[7]

What about cooks themselves? If food is spiritual, then modern 'celebrity chefs' have become our priests or gurus, druidic conduits to the ineffable. The cook is in tune with the *terroir*; an interpreter of Gaia for our lip-smacking pleasure and spiritual improvement. We no longer trust politicians or the clergy; but we are hungry for cooks to tell us not just how to eat but how to live, the moralistic synecdoche easily accomplished since we now happily accept that one lives through eating. A 2011 London Underground advert for the supermarket Waitrose reads: 'Love food. Love life.' The ordering implies a conditional: if, and only if, you love food, will you then love life, in the right way.

(A note about 'chef'. The French word 'chef' means simply boss or leader: hence our 'chief'. Its culinary sense derives from 'chef de cuisine', which means the person who runs the kitchen. Since this French borrowing seems to add an exotic mystique that contributes to our weird modern veneration of chefs, I will mainly call them 'cooks', by which I intend no personal slight. Indeed, one of the three-Michelin-stars super-chefs interviewed by Anthony Bourdain offers as his highest compliment to a rival the description: 'He's a good cook.'[8])

Gordon Ramsay, famous for being shouty and saying fuck, displays a touching empathy in one episode of his *Kitchen Nightmares* when dealing with an alcoholic cook who is going off the rails because he can't keep off the sauce; and yet the voyeuristic nature of the programme (shouldn't the poor guy be getting therapeutic help from a professional in private, rather than from a cook in public?) feels a little uncomfortable.

The Canadian Food Network's Ricardo Larrivée, 'Québec's answer to Jamie Oliver', went on a TV talk show to advise men to shave their pubic hair, a piece of lifestyle advice apparently not directly related to food-safety issues.[9] More wonkishly, Jamie Oliver himself nobly agitates for British schoolchildren to be served something better than doubtfully recombined turkey offcuts, and is afforded a parallel level of respect when, though not an educationalist, he starts issuing demands about what should happen in the classroom as well as the canteen, asking for cooking classes to be made compulsory. Lest anyone object that all these hours of chopping, boiling, and grilling might detract from the study of mathematics or Mandarin, Oliver explains that one can learn just about everything through the medium of food: cooking is 'a tool to teach other subjects such as maths, science, and art in a more fun and engaging way'.[10] One could no doubt try to build an orrery out of meatballs and spaghetti, but the idea that foodism is a kind of gateway drug to the wider world of scholarly endeavour seems optimistic. That an entrepreneur-cook's thoughts on education policy should revolve around food is not surprising; that people should take them seriously is. Nor is Oliver a doctor or public-health-policy scholar, yet the media solicits his expert comment on the government's new 'obesity plan' all the same.[11]

He is not formally elected, yet Jamie Oliver is in a way democratically chosen by all the people who watch his TV programmes and buy his book-shaped products. Perhaps celebrity foodists are the leaders we now deserve. Some of them certainly appear to think so. The 'Lima Declaration' or 'Open Letter to the Chefs of Tomorrow', launched by René Redzepi (of recently anointed 'world's best restaurant' Noma in Copenhagen) with the Spanish cook Ferran Adrià of El Bulli and other famous aproned friends in 2011, announces that cooking is 'more than the search for happiness'; indeed it is a 'transformative tool' that 'can change the way the world nourishes itself' (not merely, it is implied, by spraying froth at a few rich people). A cook ought to be 'socially engaged, conscious of and responsible for his or her contribution to a fair and sustainable society'; and, moreover, 'through our cooking, our ethics and our aesthetics, we can contribute to the culture and identity of a people, a region, a country', and 'we all have a responsibility to know and protect nature'.[12] Only cooks, it seems, can save us from bad politics, cultural decline, and ecocidal apocalypse.

In *The Fat Duck Cookbook*, meanwhile, Heston Blumenthal indulgently reproduces the 'Statement on the "New Cookery"' that he co-wrote with Ferran Adrià, Thomas Keller, and Harold McGee in 2006, which claims that they are able to 'give pleasure and meaning to people through the medium of food'.[13] Even the most authoritarian priests of more pious ages never claimed that they gave people salvation or 'meaning' themselves, merely that these things were available only through the word of God as the robed men interpreted it. When cooks are sermonizing to the effect that it is through them that people get 'meaning', it begins to look as though the bunny-broilers are getting a Christ complex.

You might think that, to deserve the name, a person's life-'meaning' ought to transcend her function as an ambulatory digestive tract. But it turns out that, in a dizzying hermeneutic move, food can be transcendent – both of itself and of the manner of its gobbling. So argues the philosophically ambitious statement by Thomas Keller, of the much-worshipped French Laundry restaurant in California, that 'Preparing tripe [. . .] is a transcendental act: to take what is normally thrown away and, with skill and knowledge, turn it into something exquisite.'[14] Perhaps there is, after all, something transcendentally recursive about putting another animal's intestines into your own, something titillatingly reminiscent of the Ouroboros or Möbius strip. We could perhaps attain even greater transcendence by following the example of the Roman emperor Commodus, who, according to the *Historia Augusta*, 'often mixed human excrement with the most expensive foods, and did not refrain from tasting them'.[15]

The modern hunger to accord food 'meaning' and even transcendentalism seems a relatively recent development: it is refreshing to note the absence of such inflated claims, for example, in the much-loved 1931 American cookbook *The Joy of Cooking*, by Irma Rombauer. Her rhetoric hits a modest peak in the introductory remarks: 'This book is the result of a long practical experience, a lively curiosity and a real love for cookery. In it I have made an attempt to meet the needs of the average household, to make palatable dishes with simple means and to lift everyday cooking out of the commonplace.'[16] Cooking here is an enjoyable act, perhaps one even worthy of a certain 'love'; and the author's aim is to help you cook nicer food, every day. What could be more civilized?

Yet since then foodist rhetoric has, like the early universe, experienced a period of rapid inflation. The foodist movement is desperate to claim other cultural domains as inherent virtues of food itself, so as not ever to have to stop thinking about stuffing its face. So food becomes, as we shall see, not only spiritual nourishment but art, sex, ecology, history, fashion, and ethics. It even becomes, in the mind of some of its more addled fanatics, a universal language. Alex James, for instance, told the *Sun*: 'Food is a brilliant way to connect with anyone. I used to think music was a universal language. But if you go to Africa and play a Blur song, someone might have to translate. Give them cheese, though, and they can instantly taste it and react.'[17] And so a hunk of Cheddar becomes superior to *Nevermind*: a universal medium of communication; or at least, for foodists, a universal solvent of the intellect.

Even Maya Angelou, possessed of more literary credibility than Alex James, says: 'Writing and cookery are just two different means of communication.'[18] Perhaps she would say this while promoting her new cookbook (*Great Food, All Day Long*), but it's still a strange conflation of activities with wholly different purposes. In *Le Cru et le Cuit* (*The Raw and the Cooked*), Lévi-Strauss argues that the discovery of cooking meat with fire was the beginning of our humanity, and analyses cooking techniques as a meaning-system, but that does not mean that cooking is actually a language. You cannot 'communicate' ideas through cookery, just as you cannot communicate bodily nourishment through writing. What cookery really communicates, in the original sense of that word 'to make public', is: food. But from the shady assertion that food can 'give meaning', it is only a short step to saying that this meaning can be artistic: in short, that food itself can be art.

3.

The Hunger Artists

'These are just some olives we picked up from the market today,' comments the waiter casually, as he places a tiny bowl containing two very large and very green-looking olives on our table. I bite into one and my brain short-circuits, unable to process the contradictory signals, until the taste resolves into something oddly sweet and fruity. Another waiter passes by and chucklingly informs us that the 'olives' are actually stuffed kumquats. Touché.

Over a three-hour lunch, my companion and I also experience a chalky garlic chestnut, a small oblong of trout with appley potato noodles, a crab croquette, some blowtorched mullet with 'shaved cured egg yolks', a pile of seeds 'smoked over hay', a prawn (rather lonely) with mushrooms on a stone, a bit of salt cod (a version of bacalhau), two slices of rare pigeon with red cabbage and chocolate sauce, and a tiny sandwich of chicken parfait, in the middle of which is concealed (surprise!) a slice of hard-boiled egg.

Not to forget the iced cucumber, some chewy mandarin ice cream, a mushroomy chocolate truffle (a pun, my friend astutely observes, on two senses of 'truffle'), and what my notes describe as 'Roast celeriac & shaving foam'. Near the end a waiter arrives with a couple of what look like dry-ice-sweating sugared almonds. 'I'll have to ask you to have this straight away, because it's frozen,' he commands sternly. Obediently, I close my mouth around what turns out to be a bolus of vanilla-infused olive oil, which has been frozen with liquid nitrogen. It's very . . . oily.

All this food is served prettily on slates or stones or rectangular plates, with crafty splashes of colour and obscure garnishing leaves, and it is extraordinarily elaborate and inventive. Is it, perhaps, art? That's what some people claim, at least, about this style of cooking, known as 'molecular gastronomy'. We are in the fashionably Scandinavian dining room of Viajante, the London restaurant of cook Nuno Mendes, who worked under Ferran Adrià at El Bulli. To eat through its six-course tasting menu, bookended by blizzards of amuse-bouches and petits fours, makes for a fascinating experience, if not a really satisfying lunch. It bears the same relationship to a meal as a showreel of special-effects demos does to a film.

In 1932, Salvador Dalí exhibited in Paris his 'hypnagogic clock', which he described as 'an enormous loaf of bread posed on a luxurious pedestal'. He also conceived a splendid project for a 'secret society of bread', in which giant loaves (fifteen to forty-five metres long) would be left anonymously in public locations in Paris or New York City. In this way, Dalí theorized, 'one could subsequently try to ruin systematically the logical meaning of all the mechanisms of the rational practical world'.[1]

Sadly, the secret society of bread remained entirely conceptual. For the foodist, in any case, food is already art. As one of the early manifestos of modern foodism, 1984's *The Official Foodie Handbook*, put it: 'Foodies consider food to be an art, on a level with painting or drama. It's actually your *favourite* art form.'[2] Now such talk is everywhere, serenely unconscious of its own hyperbole. Bernard Loiseau's $60 frogs' legs are 'a dazzling show of artistry'.[3] Anthony Bourdain heretically refers to Ferran Adrià as 'this foam guy',[4] but others are bewitched by the Spaniard's aesthetic froth: Adrià's foam is 'incredibly beautiful [. . .] like a piece of art';[5] and his 'wild genius in the kitchen is often likened to that of Salvador Dalí in the art world'.[6] (Adrià is not known, at the time of this writing, to have secreted enormous baguettes in major cities.) You can now get the Nigella Quick Collection app for your iPad, which the launch PR said 'curates' her meals,[7] as though they were canvases or installation pieces.

The idea that food is an 'art form' in itself is a much stronger claim than traditional phrasing such as 'the art of cookery' (on the model of the French *l'art de . . .*), a more modest attribution of creativity and craft (*techné* rather than *poésis*) to quotidian activity. Now, the top cooks are sounding positively petulant about a supposed lack of artistic recognition: 'If an artist or a musician can generate emotions from painting and music,' Heston Blumenthal wonders, 'why can't a chef do the same with food?'[8] Everyone wants to be a rock star. (Even as rock star Josh Homme, of Queens of the Stone Age, eagerly tells *Q* magazine that he and his friend Dave Grohl like sushi: 'We're very foodist' – thus happily sanctioning my preferred term.)[9] Indeed, the cooks and their foodist acolytes conspire together in the elevation of cook to the status of Axl Rose, Anish Kapoor or Thelonius Monk. The cook is said to 'interpret' old dishes, as an instrumentalist or conductor interprets a piece from the repertoire. ('This is pastry chef Stephen Durfee's interpretation of a traditional strudel.')[10] Appeals are made to the 'meaning' or even to the 'emotion' allegedly induced by the scoffing of elaborate food. Hervé This, one of the early theorists of 'molecular gastronomy', reserves his admiration for 'inspired' cooks, whose 'objective is not to fill up the stomachs of their guests, but to produce culinary art'.[11] You might go hungry, but you had better weep and applaud.

The British food historian Christopher Driver, who was also the inaugural editor of the *Guardian*'s food pages, writes that food can be art because 'both simple and complex combinations of food and drink are capable of engaging the intelligence as well as the appetites and feelings'.[12] To say that a thing is 'capable of engaging the intelligence', however, is to get things the wrong way round, attributing agency to the object of study so as to valorize it. The truth is that the intelligence can be directed at anything at all: it is omnivorous. But some things might be more nutritious for it than others. The former Microsoft executive and now patent-litigation entrepreneur Nathan Myhrvold, for example, is no doubt a very intelligent man, but he still exhibits a curiously pleading tone. 'If music can be art, why can't food?' Myhrvold whines.[13] It should be obvious that a steak is not like a symphony, a pie not like a passacaglia, foie gras not like a fugue; that the 'composition' of a menu is not like the composition of a requiem; that the cook heating things in the kitchen and arranging them on a plate is not the artistic equal of Charlie Parker. But then, I wouldn't necessarily trust Ozzy Osbourne or Mozart to cook my dinner. The practices are simply different. Myhrvold is bound to engage in such inflation of food's value, though, because he is plugging his own new six-volume, million-word cookbook, ominously entitled *Modernist Cuisine*, which costs £395.

Interviewed on the BBC's *Food Programme*, Myhrvold described himself and the top art-cooks as a beleaguered minority who are misunderstood by the people who bring 'ideological principles' to food, although it is in fact the foodists like Myhrvold himself who are the ideological mainstream in our day. He even went so far as to compare the supposed modern distrust of experimental art-foodism with the scandalized reception of the Impressionists in nineteenth-century Paris. 'But today the same paintings – the Monet water-lilies and the Cézanne still-lifes – are the best-loved art in the world,' he finished triumphantly.[14] This is a splendidly paradigmatic example of what is known as the Van Gogh fallacy: because I am despised and rejected by the 'establishment', I must be a genius. (Far from being rejected by the establishment, in any case, Ferran Adrià – who developed techniques including 'making a tomato explode with a bicycle pump' – and Myrhvold's other heroes are fêted by the establishment incessantly.)[15]

Food is a plastic medium, and you can sculpt things out of it, as every toddler knows. Perhaps that makes food art, and cooks rock-star sculptors? One of an earlier age's celebrity chefs, the pâtissier Marie-Antoine Carême (who was active in the early nineteenth century and is credited with inventing the toque, or chef's hat) certainly thought so. As Heston Blumenthal writes admiringly, Carême made 'models of classic temples, rotundas and bridges rendered in fastidious detail in marzipan, pork fat and pastry, decorated with spun sugar or fruits [. . .] At one dinner for forty people given by the Prince Regent in Brighton Pavilion, a first course of forty-eight dishes was followed by eight Carême creations, including a "Chinese Hermitage" and "The Ruin of the Turkish Mosque".'[16] But here food is not art, just as sand is not art even though you can build elaborate sandcastles with it. Of course, anything can be a material, and you could build a sculpture out of carrots and exhibit it successfully in a gallery. But Carême's creations, rather than proving the inherent artiness of food, seem rather to bespeak a jokish spectacularism in an orgy of conspicuous waste. (Arguably a more culturally resonant use of sculptural food is the cake that adorns the cover of *Let It Bleed* by the Rolling Stones – knocked up quickly by none other than Delia Smith, who recalls: 'They wanted it to be very over-the-top and as gaudy as I could make it.')[17]

Perhaps the new foodism can be called artistic because it is so technically inventive. Heston Blumenthal cooks with liquid nitrogen; Grant Achatz of Chicago's Alinea has 'invented a transparent rosewater envelope'; Wylie Dufresne of New York's wd-50 'invented deep-fried hollandaise, foie gras tied into a knot, and instant tofu noodles'.[18] Now, the idea that a cook should have more than a nodding acquaintance with science is not new: the nineteenth-century celebrity chef Alexis Soyer, who cooked at London's Reform Club and went to Crimea to improve the soldiers' food, remarked: 'To make a good cook it is of paramount importance that a man should possess some chemical as well as medical knowledge.'[19] In an update of Soyer's wartime mission, Heston Blumenthal once spent a television programme trying to convince the crew of a British Navy submarine to eat weird concoctions involving blueberries or cod's tongues before realizing, with dramatic belatedness, that they needed decent, ordinary food, and doing a 'sous vide' beef stew: not arty but hearty.[20] The fact that the Navy subsequently expressed interest in preparing all its food along the same lines shows that Heston's expertise is extremely useful when sensibly directed; indeed, he would no doubt have suggested this right off the bat were he not obliged to make an hour of television and so create some ersatz drama out of sailors refusing to eat his deliberately ridiculous dishes. (Alexis Soyer's own Crimean recipes were eminently edible things such as 'Salt Pork with Mashed Peas, for One Hundred Men'.)[21]

The cook's treadmill of enforced invention has been running a long time, too. Auguste Escoffier, the much-venerated head cook at the Paris Ritz and London Savoy a century ago, who is credited with formalizing the techniques of modern cooking in his severe 900-page manual of 1907, sighed: 'It is an exceedingly common mania among people of inordinate wealth to exact incessantly new or so-called new dishes [. . .] Novelty! It is the prevailing cry; it is imperiously demanded by everyone. [. . .] What feats of ingenuity have we not been forced to perform, at times, in order to meet our customers' wishes? Personally, I have ceased counting the nights spent in the attempt to discover new combinations.'[22] Pity, too, the modernist cook-inventors, for they eat not what they do. (When Anthony Bourdain asks around top cooks for what they would choose as their last meal, it's all regular home-cooking, nothing restaurantish.)[23] But technical creativity by itself, much as we might admire it in cooks, sound recordists, or designers of assault rifles, does not make for art either.

Perhaps cooking can be art, then, if it becomes a kind

of multimedia performance. That is the hope of Heston Blumenthal, who seemingly announces that he won't stop until cooking is considered not just the equal of but actually better than music, theatre, and everything else: 'The act of eating engages all the senses as well as the mind. Preparing and serving food could therefore be the most complex and comprehensive of the performing arts.'[24] Really? More 'complex' and 'comprehensive' than the *Oresteia* or a concert by Prince? Well, Blumenthal's lavish book of fairytale foods, *Heston's Fantastical Feasts*, does contain a house made of food, and some vertiginously conceptual dishes such as 'Deep-fried Brains-within-a-Brain', 'Chicken Testicle Jelly Beans', and 'Aerated Chocolate Door'; but it is *The Fat Duck Cookbook* that is the more interesting revelation of his artistic despotism. He wants to colonize all the diner's senses at once, with 'a dish that involved three different sound effects during eating', or squirts of perfume: 'The 2002 version of Jelly of Oyster and Passion Fruit with Lavender was for a while accompanied by a spritz of lavender essential oil from an atomiser.'[25] His seafood dish 'Sound of the Sea' is served with a conch shell containing a tiny mp3 player which plays the sound of seagulls and 'the long withdrawing roar of waves on the shore'.[26]

The allusion to Matthew Arnold's 'Dover Beach' here ('melancholy, long, withdrawing roar') perhaps unconsciously signals that Blumenthal believes his own super-elaborate foodism to be the signal of the imminent collapse of civilization. It would not be the first time that a conception of food-as-art was taken as a symptom of degraded cultural priorities. The Roman historian Livy notes the point that 'the beginnings of foreign luxury' were introduced to Rome by armies returning from Asia, who brought back with them bronze couches, fine tapestries, and a new veneration of chefs: 'The cook whom the ancients regarded and treated as the lowest menial was rising in value, and what had been a servile office came to be looked upon as a fine art.'[27] But then we must acknowledge that a moralizing suspicion of all fancy nosh, of the kind that Socrates in Plato's *Republic* affirms would only be eaten in a 'fevered' society, is often just the foodist's snobbery turned upside down.[28]

What is more interesting about Blumenthal's work is that he is reinventing, knowingly or not, the culinary ideas of the Italian Futurist Marinetti, which were collected in *The Futurist Cookbook* of 1932. Heston wonders about the affinity of sound with taste; Marinetti gives that a name ('conrumore [. . .] Example: the *conrumore* of rice in orange sauce and a motorcycle engine'),[29] and he also demands 'The use in prescribed doses of poetry and music as surprise ingredients'.[30] (In foodist Rome, 'Banquets were made more attractive by the presence of girls who played on the harp and sang and danced, and by other forms of amusement', to which no one could reasonably object.)[31] Heston has a waiter spray you with lavender; Marinetti demands: 'Every dish must be preceded by a perfume which will be driven from the table with the help of electric fans.'[32] Marinetti excites himself over the prospect of 'a battery of scientific instruments in the kitchen' including 'ozonizers' and 'ultra-violet ray lamps'; Heston's Fat Duck recipes are furnished with just such technocratic upholstery, calling for the use of liquid nitrogen and deionized water, and apparatus such as a Dewar flask and refractometer.[33] In 2009, a New York City cook named Matt Weingarten held a futurist banquet for 100 guests based on Marinetti's cookbook.[34] And so, the 'frantic love of novelty' in food denounced by Escoffier more than 100 years ago spins on. (Ferran Adrià himself has mysteriously announced the necessity for 'a new food movement every twenty or twenty-five years'. Why?)[35]

Futurist cooking was explicitly fascist in its motivation: 'The militarization of a young culture is where we find our strength,' Marinetti declared. 'Therefore we do not want Italian cooking to remain a museum.'[36] But there is a subtler kind of authoritarianism in its demand to control all aspects of the eater's experience, and that is also what Heston Blumenthal aspires to. The ambition is to make food into what Wagner called a *Gesamtkunstwerk*, a total work of art. But what if your ideal of eating a meal at a restaurant is to think and talk about something other than food, instead of sitting through some high-class musical cabaret of Langoustines on Ice?

Of course no one goes to the Fat Duck every day, and having one's senses soaked in such a foodist circus is no doubt an entertaining experience, as was my relatively less theatrical meal at Viajante. Luckily, since actually eating this stuff is so expensive, reading about it is pretty entertaining too. The recipes in Heston's *Fat Duck Cookbook* are manifestly uncookable by the average purchaser; such volumes are really a baroque species of fantasy fiction. It seems surprising, then, that so few food-as-art theorists suggest that the cookbook can approach the status of literature, which might be a more reasonable claim than that your lunch can be art. The laconic and humorous prose of guts-on-a-plate pioneer Fergus Henderson (in his book *Nose to Tail Eating*) is considerably more stylish and well crafted than that of much modern 'literary' fiction. But while everyone wants to be a rock star, not so many want to be ink-stained wretches. Or perhaps foodists do not want their 'passion' subsumed under the general rubric of writing, because then one might feel tempted to read all kinds of other diverting books on different subjects, rather than spending the whole time researching one's next dinner.

4.

Word Soup

The French writer and *nouveau romancier* Alain Robbe-Grillet relates the following scene of lunch with his friend Roland Barthes: 'In a restaurant, he said, it is the menu that people enjoy consuming – not the dishes, but their description. Lo and behold, he had relegated the whole art of cooking – which he adored – to the status of an abstract exercise of vocabulary!'[1]

But Barthes understood more than his friend. The restaurant menu is not only a kind of *poésie concrète*, as well as an enticing promise of satisfaction, an IOU for pleasurable consumption in the near future; not just, as Barthes himself wrote elsewhere, the 'syntax' of a given food 'system'; it can actually alter how we experience the food once it arrives.[2] The linguistic framing of a menu description has been shown to change what people report having tasted.

In an experiment, two psychologists gave different groups of people Heston Blumenthal's 'Crab Ice Cream' while describing it differently: one group was told it was about to eat a 'savoury mousse', the other was expecting 'ice cream'. The people given savoury mousse liked it, but the people thinking they were eating ice cream found it 'digusting' and even 'the most unpleasant food they had ever tasted'.[3] (In the same way, my kumquat cunningly misdescribed as an olive at Viajante tasted very weird indeed.) The psychologists add that most food tastes 'blander' without the 'expectation of flavour caused by the visual appearance or verbal description of what is going to be eaten'. One is reminded of Terry Gilliam's film *Brazil*, in which the plates of homogeneous brown muck at the restaurant are differentiated by the colour photos stuck in them and the savouring announcement of their names: 'Numero deux, duck à l'orange', 'Numero une, crevettes à la mayonnaise'. (The philosopher Slavoj Žižek comments: 'This split between the food's image and the real of its formless excremental remainder perfectly exemplifies the disintegration of reality into an interface image, ghostlike and insubstantial.')[4] The 'exercise of vocabulary' in a menu, then, is never merely 'abstract', as Robbe-Grillet thought. You eat their words.

For some examples of the modern state of the art in gastrolinguistic engineering, let us consider L'Enclume, the Michelin-starred restaurant in the English Lake District, and its bill of fare as advertised on its website in November 2011. As a literary-gustatory experiment, I'm going simply to read the menu without investigating further, so attempting empathetically to recreate the literary experience of the diner who has just sat down and read the dish descriptions, and is thereby set off on a pleasurable trail of wondering what exactly it is that he might end up eating. The first dish I propose for our imaginative consideration is this: 'Carrot sacks with brawn and juniper, fried cake and cress'. It is surely a masterpiece of tantalizing obscurity. I confess to having no idea what 'carrot sacks' are: probably not the kind of coarse hessian sack in which one might transport twenty kilos of carrots, but then what? Tiny pretend bags made out of thin shavings of carrot artfully woven together? This dish also features 'fried cake', which has me pondering the dubious desirability of frying a chocolate or sponge cake, but that cannot be it. Could it be a fishcake? Who knows? Again, I purpose not to discover the truth, lest the effect of phantastical stupefaction be ruined in any reader of this text who subsequently makes the gastronomic voyage to the restaurant itself.

One thing I do know is that 'brawn' is pâté made from a pig's head: the name is an obvious example of menu euphemism. Verbs tend to ascribe benign agency to the parts of a dead animal, as with the announcement by the waiter at L'Enclume who, in Steve Coogan and Rob Brydon's television series *The Trip*, introduces a dish thus: 'You've got some little manx queenies which are baby queen scallops. They're resting on grilled baby gem and parsley coulis as well as a light creamy horseradish sauce.' When the waiter leaves, Brydon comments: 'Rather optimistic to say they're "resting". Their days of resting have been and gone. They are dead.'[5] (*The Trip* is, among other things, a wonderful satire on foodism, and the zeitgeisty truth that eating expensive food is now what middle-aged men do together: indeed, two men of my acquaintance went on a *The Trip* trip, eating in some of the same restaurants, and learned from one arch waiter that they were far from alone in their pilgrimage.) Even more cutely, animal parts are often said to be doing their 'resting' on a 'bed' (of spinach, or parsley coulis, as it might be), waiting for the eater to spear them, in a kind of sexual reverie of anticipated violence, like heaving-breasted heroines leaving their window open for Count Dracula.

It is an interesting question, meanwhile, why the word 'baby' in menu descriptions does not disgust us. Surely the last things we want to eat are babies. But perhaps once we are lulled into an imaginative world where a 'baby' lamb or the 'baby' queen scallop can be 'resting' (in the scallop's case, resting itself on another baby, this time a 'baby gem', since vegetables too – baby carrots, baby greens – can share in the general babyhood of all nice things, and participate in tottering towers of babies all stacked up for our gastric enjoyment), we are cocooned in such a euphemistic dream that the incipient act of putting these 'baby' organisms into our mouths doesn't register as the horrific dissonance it otherwise might. Babies are often pictured as smiling and trusting, which is perhaps one reason why calling pieces of food 'babies' makes them sound more amiable and unthreatening.

Another dish on offer at L'Enclume is this: 'Rare breed pork and crispy skin, salsify, onions and hedge garlic'. (As with almost all of the menu, there is no clue to how any of this was cooked. At least we knew in the previous dish that the 'cake' was fried. But how did this skin get so crispy? Is it even pork skin? Perhaps it is the blowtorched epidermis of an ocelot.) Whenever I am confronted with the promise of eating 'rare breed' pig, I do suffer some ecological anxiety. If these animals are so rare, should we really be eating them? Might they not be gobbled extinct by nihilistic gastromaniacs? There is no guarantee, anyway, that a 'rare breed' will taste better than a common one; a 'rare breed' might be an evolutionary blunder, a porcine DNA dead end. Perhaps it is rare for a very good reason. Happily, Sudi Pigott, author of the extraordinary foodist manual *How to Be a Better Foodie*, explains: 'This doesn't mean pedigree breeds are about to become extinct – quite the reverse – they're undergoing a much-needed revival.'[6] The coming paradox: once a formerly 'rare' breed becomes common as muck thanks to all the foodists flocking to pig out on it, restaurants will have to stop calling it 'rare' and we will instead be invited, perhaps, to chew on 'vintage pig'. (Another dish at L'Enclume does, spectacularly, promise 'vintage potatoes'.) What, meanwhile, is 'hedge garlic'? It conjures the amusingly bucolic image of bulbs of garlic hanging in a hedge, swinging wild and free in the English country wind, but actually – all right, I looked it up – it denotes a green plant (*Alliaria petiolata*) that is often found next to hedges, and has also gloried in the names 'Jack-by-the-hedge' and 'Poor Man's Mustard', though one can immediately see why an expensive restaurant wouldn't choose to use that last moniker. (I didn't come here to eat a poor man's anything.)

The air of comfortingly expensive discrimination afforded by the precise description attains a new level of art here: 'Gott's Holker milk-fed spring lamb, sheep's milk curds, turnips, ramsons'. Well, obviously no one in the world knows what ramsons are. (Answer: 'wild garlic' or 'wood garlic' or 'bear's garlic' – a garlicky member of the onion family, related to chives.) Now, a word about 'spring lamb'. It used to be the case that a 'spring lamb' was a lamb you ate in spring. The old English breed of Dorset Horn ewes gave birth in the autumn, which gave the lambs just enough time to grow over the winter and be scoffed at Eastertime. But most breeds of sheep actually give birth in the spring, so a spring lamb from those mothers ought to be eaten in the winter.[7] Confusingly, now people want to scarf 'spring lamb' all year round, so in the industry a 'spring lamb' means nothing more than a lamb 'raised on grass and butchered at the right weight rather than a certain time of year'.[8] All this makes the designation 'spring lamb' entirely unreliable except as a spur to a cheerful mental image of the meat on your plate having gambolled happily over the meadows in at least one calendar April, somewhere on the planet.

L'Enclume's 'spring lamb' is also 'milk-fed', which is

reassuring, because you don't want to eat one of those lambs that are force-fed only ground-up cow skeletons and spongiform panda brains. The 'Gott's Holker' part, meanwhile, which could perhaps pass for the exclamation of a hungry German, is the precise kind of milk-fed spring lamb we are talking about, and turns out to mean (fine, I gave in and looked this up too) a sheep from Holker Farm, which is run by a sheep farmer and sheep's cheesemonger named Martin Gott. Hence, 'Gott's Holker milk-fed spring lamb'. So tastily named, I am sure it is the more delicious for it.

An alternative trend in menu language is the objectivist use of scientific terminology, in the wake of such Heston Blumenthal concoctions as 'Nitro-Poached Green Tea and Lime Mousse':[9] so, for example, the 'scallops in caper emulsion' offered at Hipping Hall, Brent Hulena's restaurant in Cumbria. Emulsion is the new cutting-edge replacement for 'drizzle' ('drizzled with oil', passim), but one day we will be bored of emulsions too – as well as all the 'suspensions, gels, aerosols' that the forward-thinking Hervé This already considers tedious,[10] and something even newer will be required to pique our interest. Hervé himself offers an exciting clue: 'Let us [. . .] observe that nature produces no fruit, vegetable, meat, or fish in the shape of a pyramid. In choosing this visual form, we will avoid comparison to other classic foods.'[11] Someone give the man a bar of Toblerone.

On the other hand, a menu can afford to go for a style that is as simple as possible, almost purely list-like, if it is confident of the inherent shock value offered by weird combinations of ingredients. Thus the tasting menu at Grant Achatz's Chicago restaurant Alinea has featured dishes such as 'bubble gum, long pepper, hibiscus and crème fraîche' (served pseudoscientifically in a kind of test tube); though its menu as of late 2011 seems sober by comparison, its most unusual ingredient being an 'explosion'. (The headline ingredient and dish name, 'BLACK TRUFFLE', is followed by a fuzzy grey circle and then the words 'explosion, romaine, parmesan'.)[12] Perhaps this is a little joke on the cliché about 'an explosion of favour' (restaurant critics, passim), or a description of the way the truffle has been cleverly extruded all over the plate. But a dining experience that actually featured blowing stuff up would have a rather Ride of the Valkyries vim to it. (Perhaps Heston Blumenthal is currently experimenting with the 'emotion' that can be induced with the careful application of C4 and hand grenades.) Oh, all right, I looked that up as well: the dish is a single 'raviolo' served in a spoon, and according to one food blogger's description, 'It did actually explode in your mouth':[13] here, of course, 'actually' means 'not', like the modern use of 'literally' to mean 'metaphorically'. (My tiny chicken-parfait sandwich at Viajante was, I think, called 'Thai explosion II'. Needless to say, nothing exploded.)

Sometimes, though, a foodstuff just sounds inherently disgusting, so it has to be rebranded. The *New York Times* restaurant critic Ruth Reichl recounts having made the scales fall from the eyes of an annoying fellow diner: 'I know you

ordered Chilean sea bass [. . .] but there is no such thing.
You are eating Patagonian toothfish [. . .] it didn't sell very
well under its own name. So they changed it.'[14] Having thus
been rebranded as the 'Chilean sea bass' in the 1970s, though
it was not actually a sea bass, the animal became so popular
that it was eventually fished nearly to collapse, as also began
to happen in the same decade when the 'slimehead fish' was
remarketed as the exotic 'orange roughy'. The 'goosefish'
suddenly leapt in popularity during the mid-1980s when it
was renamed 'monkfish'. And now catfish is sold in the US
under the new name 'delacata'.[15]

Bearing in mind the crab-ice-cream psychology experiments
mentioned at the start of this chapter, it seems probable that
giving a fish a new name actually makes it taste better, as
well as making it easier to sell – if it sounds more palatable,
it will be. But a dish might also be renamed, tragically, to
erase the taint of thoughtcrime. The Turkish dish 'cigarette
borek' (*sigara boregi*) is a fried pastry filled with feta cheese and
parsley, so called because it is long and thin, like a cigarette.
Unfortunately in these times one mustn't mention cigarettes
at all, lest the very word be allowed to work its devilish
power on innocent pastry-scoffers who have never previously
even heard of the existence of smokable tobacco packages
and turn them at one fell swoop into hollow-eyed nicotine
junkies. So, the public-health-minded Union of Restaurant
Owners in the city of Adapazari held a meeting about how to
remove this noxious propaganda, and decided in their wisdom

that henceforth the pastry should instead be called a 'pencil borek'.[16] It remains to be seen whether sales of Turkish pencils soar – as, if the puritan pastry purifiers are correct, they must.

Lest all the artifice of breed descriptions, chemistry-set jargon, and ingredient rebranding in the posher kind of restaurant make a certain kind of diner suspicious, a parallel recent trend is the reassuring adjective 'proper'. It appears everywhere on gastropub menus ('proper pork pie', 'proper mash'), in one-up-from-McDonald's burger joints ('proper hamburgers', promises the London chain Byron), and in the mellifluously matey warbling of Jamie Oliver munching a Vietnamese Banh Minh in an East End market ('That is a proper, proper sandwich'),[17] and his own dish names: 'Proper Bloke's Sausage Fusilli', 'Roast of Incredible Game Birds with Proper Polenta'.[18] The use of 'proper' anticipates and indulges (even implants) a suspicion of fanciness, whether it is owed to dubious foreign practices or modern industrial adulteration. It is also one of the favourite epithets employed by Britain's shiny-jowled Prime Minister, David Cameron: 'proper politics', 'proper punishment', 'proper immigration control'. 'Proper' here works as a strategy to avoid seeming privileged, while at the same time tuning in cunningly to anti-intellectual prejudice (what is 'proper' is not over-thought), all as Cameron conducts, like some kind of over-moisturized Visigoth, his philistine economic campaign against the BBC, universities ('proper education'), and the National Health Service ('proper healthcare'). Just as one ought to be suspicious of the word 'proper' when hoarsely brayed from the glistening lips of David Cameron, one ought to be suspicious of it on a menu: is it anything more than a vatic invocation of old-school purity?

Sometimes the exquisite balance of the menu must be betrayed for commercial reasons. Hence the wonderfully distempered outburst by Marco Pierre White on the 'Chocolate Assiette' he sold at his restaurant Harvey's, a sugary compendium of white-chocolate sorbet, dark-chocolate mousse, raspberry mousse, chocolate sauce and 'sheeting', and hot chocolate soufflé, garnished with orange zest, raspberries, and mint leaves. White comments: 'This is disgusting; it's a horrible dish. It's vulgarity pure and simple. It's a dish invented for suburbia; it should be called "Chocolate Suburbia". Why do we serve it? Because we're commercial. Because, at the end of the day, you have to please the customer. And this does.'[19] With that in mind, one can appreciate all the more the terrifically economical sarcasm that White has invested in the dish's title, playing on the extra tang of sophistication implicit in calling it an 'assiette' rather than a mere 'plate'.

A menu dish name, then, can even sneer, as well as promising gustatory pleasure, interesting mouthfeel, communion with nature, ethical responsibility, science at your service, relaxed and willing sacrificial meat, and a fish that does not sound trashy; and in doing all this it attributes, very flatteringly, subtle powers of discrimination to the prospective eater himself. As a literary artefact the menu is powerful indeed:

a psychic amuse-gueule. No surprise, then, that someone should hit on the wheeze of making the menu a literal amuse-gueule as well. So at Alinea in Chicago, for example, one may, after reading the menu, eat it, because it has been made with lasers, liquid nitrogen, and ink-jet printers. Perhaps the edible menu is to dining what edible knickers are to sex. Tactfully, I will leave the elaboration of that analogy as an exercise for the reader.

5.

Sex on a Plate

Sticky fingers don't do it any more; now you need a sticky face too. In December 2011, a photograph of Nigella Lawson with salted caramel running down her fizzog for the cover of *Stylist* magazine had Twitter hyperventilating. Nigella archly denied that there was anything sexualized about the image – 'it is simply rapturous joy in caramel' – though a sceptic might point out that the joy most people take in caramel results from gobbling it rather than tipping it over their heads for the watching cameras. No doubt it would be smutty to read the brown goo splashed over Nigella's face as a deliberate analogue of the white goo splashed over the face of a female porn actor, though the caramel picture, too, is nothing if not a money shot.

Nigella herself boldly denied that she trafficked in 'double entendre', which in a way is true: the sex chat of her TV food-cabaret is not really subtle enough to count as double entendre. It's more like entendre et demi. ('Ah, look at these gorgeous golden globules'; 'My mouth can handle it all.') But Nigella is just the most knowing, vampish performer in a ubiquitous passion play. Everyone revels in the 'filthiness' of what they are naughtily pleased to call 'gastroporn', congratulating themselves on their own delicious sinfulness while at the same time denying that there is anything wrong with it.

Modern foodists have not invented the link between food and sex – the 'pleasures of the oral cavity', as B.R. Myers puts it with jokey anhedonism, are after all multifarious – but they don't half go on about it.[1] One might almost suspect that this is because, bloated and obsessed with food, they aren't actually getting all that much physical love, even if they are always committed to swallowing. That they attempt to fill this void with even more food is suggested by a passage in *Eat, Pray, Love* in which Elizabeth Gilbert wakes up in the middle of the night 'with a heavy sigh and a physical hunger so deep I didn't have any idea of how to satisfy it'. So she makes herself some fried potatoes, 'asking my body the whole while if it would please accept the satisfaction of a pound of fried potatoes in lieu of the fulfillment of lovemaking'. No, says her body, so she goes back to bed and – 'Well. A word about masturbation, if I may.'[2] As though her entire book up until that point has been about anything but masturbation, of various foodist and spiritual kinds.

Certain foods have long had a reputation for being aphrodisiac. But, it seems, *post coitum omne animal triste est* applies as much to sexualized eating as to sex itself. Indeed, after a 'Pantagruelian' tasting-menu dinner at a foodist Mecca such as the French Laundry, Anthony Bourdain informs us, no one wants to have sex; instead the happy foodist will be 'farting and belching like a medieval friar [. . .] Struggling mightily to not spray truffle-flecked chunks into the toilet'.[3] Well, indeed: if music be the food of love, it follows that food itself be not. (As Jay Rayner points out, casting a sceptical eye over a new book touted as *The Aphrodisiac Encyclopaedia*: 'There is only one truly ingestible aphrodisiac and that's the grape, after it's fermented.')[4]

It is one thing to point out that food is, perhaps, a more reliable and safer pleasure (occasional bouts of E. coli or shellfish poisoning notwithstanding) than sex: it occurs more often for most people, and according to modern mores it is more normal to enjoy it in large groups. Furthermore, you need to eat (but not to have sex) just in order to stay alive. So why not enjoy it? Sure. But it is another thing overtly to sexualize one's gluttony, a practice that quickly comes to look like a desperate kind of compensation. Nigel Slater's *Toast*, an over-buttered crumpet of a memoir of childhood food, takes pains to assure the reader near the end that, working as a young hotel cook, he was shagging every night; yet Slater nevertheless reserves the swellings of eroticized language for a description of the first time he ate gratin dauphinois: 'Warm, soft and creamy [. . .] this was food that was pure sex.'[5]

'Is every aspect of the oral system assimilated in the

kiss?' wondered Jacques Derrida, in his 1990 seminar 'Manger l'autre' ('Eating the Other').[6] Foodists are not so philosophical. 'Oral sex is the Foodies' favourite kind – good practice,' the *Official Foodie Handbook* squeaks,[7] though if you are practising oral sex like you are eating, you are probably doing at least one of them wrong. But even as a joke, the idea that sex is merely good 'practice' for eating is revealing. The prevailing idea is that eating is better sex than sex is. Anthony Bourdain gleefully describes a secret New York foodist seance in which the assembled luminaries are served the notorious ne plus ultra of the gourmet, ortolan. The ortolan bunting is a very small songbird – 'about the size of a young girl's fist', says *Le Figaro*'s restaurant critic, in a perhaps too-revealing choice of comparison – which traditionally is captured, held in a dark box and force-fed with millet over several days, and then drowned alive in armagnac before being roasted. The lucky diner eats it whole, crunching down on the tiny bones (like 'hazelnuts', says our man from *Le Fig*), with a napkin placed over his head and face so that God does not witness his disgusting gluttony. (François Mitterrand ate one for his last meal; it is now illegal in France.)[8] Bourdain reports that at the secret New York tasting, the eaters, after crunching and swallowing their baby fowls and removing the napkins from their heads, all have 'glazed, blissed-out expressions, the beginnings of guilty smiles, an identical just-fucked look on every face'.[9] Yes, they have just been fucked by tiny birds. (Maybe only hippy performance art can really get to the bottom of the sex-food nexus, as with Carolee Schneeman's 1964 piece 'Meat Joy', in which 'performers rolled nude on the floor in a display of orgiastic pleasure, covering themselves with shreds of paper, paint, sausages, fish, and chicken'.)[10]

Sexual metaphors are pandemic in restaurant reviewing, one of the more ingenious having been dreamed up by John Walsh, whose fantasy seems a cannibalistic version of one of the diarist-politician Alan Clark's conquests: a dish of rump and shoulder 'offered a brilliant contrast, as if you were eating both mother and daughter in the same dish'.[11] To be fair, restaurant criticism is the kind of challenging exercise that encourages such flights of fancy, if only to fill up the column inches. (As the novelist Sebastian Faulks wrote of his own brief stint as a restaurant critic: 'Of course, I couldn't actually write down what it had been like. You can't make "fine" run to 1,000 words.')[12] The best restaurant reviewer I have encountered in my research is the dashing Lieutenant-Colonel Newnham-Davis, who wrote about London restaurants for the *Pall Mall Gazette* in the late nineteenth century. He approached the discipline by writing simply about the food ('The quails were a trifle over-cooked'), and with vivid wit about his pseudonymous dinner companions: an annoying 'Comedian', a complaining 'Epicure', a 'facetious stockbroker friend'; and (on evidently more pleasant occasions) a pretty débutante, 'Brighteyes', or an Italian aristocrat, 'La Princesse Lointaine'. Some of his economical scene-setting is quite gorgeous. At the Hans Crescent Hotel, 'The band had been making music for the past half-hour in the winter-garden [. . .] under the rosy lamps and the palms. The violins played with a delightful softness, the rings of cigarette smoke curled and vanished up towards the glass dome.'[13]

Newnham-Davis is never so ungallant as to call a dish 'sexy', but Jamie Oliver calls his food little else ('a beautiful sexy little pasta'), as though unsure whether he would like to shag it or eat it.[14] (Perhaps the same indecision haunts devoted fans of open-mouthed 'goddess' Nigella Lawson.) And Marco Pierre White makes the interesting admission: 'A lobster is more beautiful to me than most women are.'[15] It doesn't stop him boiling them.

If food and eating are sex, then depictions of food are pornography. Hence the term 'gastroporn', which might have been coined by the journalist Alexander Cockburn in a 1977 review-essay on cookbooks in the *New York Review of Books*. Reading a book by the French chef Paul Bocuse, Cockburn calls it a 'costly [. . .] exercise in gastro-porn', and traces structural parallels between the cookbook and the sex manual: 'the same studious emphasis on leisurely technique, the same apostrophes to the ultimate, heavenly delights'.[16]

An earlier equation of representations of food and eating with porn was made by the American thriller-writer Max Ehrlich, in his 1972 novel *The Edict*. In a dystopian future, the population of Earth has swollen to 20 billion, generating a global food crisis (calories are strictly rationed) and prompting the titular edict by 'WorldGov' that outlaws procreation. Having children is punishable by death; instead, women are drugged and given animatronic doll babies. In one scene the heroine, Carole (who has had a real baby), flees from a pursuer into a 'Vistarama Theater' which is showing a 'Foodie': a historical film about the abundance of food in bygone times. There is footage of fresh vegetables in a twentieth-century supermarket, a family eating a juicy joint of roast beef, and then a 'montage of eating': 'The Foodie had been designed to titillate, and it did. What the audience saw now was not simple greed. It was pornographic. Closeups of mouths were shown, teeth grinding, juice dribbling down chins.'[17] Ehrlich's pulpish mélange of Orwell and Huxley is here rather prescient, though he wasn't to know that one day soon we would all be glorying in just such scenes of gastroporn not out of nostalgic pangs for a vanished era of abundance, but even as abundance still obtained for most of the audience.

Paul Bocuse, whose book Cockburn labelled 'gastroporn', was one of the central figures in the 'nouvelle cuisine' movement, which put a new emphasis on making grub look pretty, or 'plate art', and has therefore been credited with kicking off modern media foodism: photogenic food looked tasty in newspaper colour supplements.[18] An artistic movement in itself, with dedicated food photographers and 'stylists', visual gastroporn had its aesthetic phases: by the mid-1980s, for example, its artistes were 'experimenting with half-eaten platefuls, crumby tablecloths, the cigarette that bears a Foodie's traces'.[19] And just as airbrushes and latterly Photoshop worked unreal 'improvements' on still-image pornography, gastroporn photography had its own deceptive tricks. ('Fruit, vegetables, ice-cream and ice cubes photograph better if made in wax; a British woman makes these: £10 to £20 for a pod of peas.')[20]

Today, food imagery can adopt the shiny, eerily perfect look, like the plastified corpses of German scientist Gunther von Hagens, in tight close-up (*The Fat Duck Cookbook*); the exquisite *nature morte* with coarse linen and antique cutlery (*Miss Dahl's Voluptuous Delights*); or the semi-abstract look, with rows of apples or other produce filling the whole frame to resemble the non-representational decorations of the Alhambra (Marco Pierre White's *White Heat*). There is also the quasi-pornography of domestic contentment, spiced with the subliminal promise of sex: the cookbooks by Gwyneth Paltrow and Sophie Dahl feature innumerable shots of these women with eyes demurely downcast while they subserviently chop or pour. Paltrow's *Notes from My Kitchen* shows her thoughtfully depodding peas, a tea towel artfully slung over one shoulder, or tastefully slumming it in jovial knitwear, while the text offers seductive glimpses of the celebrity-foodist lifestyle: one dish Gwyneth discovered 'at Nora Ephron's house'; another is what she likes to serve 'when my favourite vegetarian friend, Stella McCartney, brings her family over'.[21] *Miss Dahl's Voluptuous Delights*, for its part, does not neglect finally to reward the patient reader with a subliminal analogue to the pornographic money shot: through the entire book, Dahl has been looking down or away from whatever she is doing – in a little summer cardigan smashing a crab's claw with a mallet, or spooning something out of a measuring jug to make 'Peasant Soup', looking nothing like a peasant – until in the very last photograph she is pictured sitting at the kitchen table with her hands coquettishly clasped at an angle, looking directly into the camera with an enormous, satisfied smile.

Gastroporn need not be visual: like pornography, it may be written too. Anthony Bourdain is both an enthusiastic practitioner and sharp diagnostician of the art. 'Writing about sights and sounds and flavors that might otherwise be described as orgiastic – and doing it in a way that is calculated to inspire prurient interest, lust, and envy in others . . . that raises more questions in my mind as to . . . I don't know . . . the moral dimension,' he muses, ellipses straining to maintain the casual-hip pose (for Bourdain is fundamentally a serious, and seriously good, writer).[22] A similar ambivalence between celebrating sensual delights and worrying about the decorum of such celebration has long been evident in the literary evocation of all kinds of physical pleasure. Bourdain makes a passing reference to 'Zola, the greatest of food pornographers',[23] and indeed Zola's description of the charcuterie, in The Belly of Paris, is a classic instance of literary having one's cake and eating it. Our hero Florent stares gobsmacked at the window display:

There were vast quantities of rich, succulent things, things that melted in the mouth [. . .] boned hams, nicely rounded, golden with breadcrumbs [. . .] stuffed Strasbourg tongues, with their red, varnished look [. . .] strings of black pudding coiled like harmless snakes; andouilles piled up in twos and bursting with health [. . .] pies, hot from the oven [. . .] great cuts of veal and pork, whose jelly was as limpid as crystallized sugar [. . .] strings of sausages and saveloys hung down symmetrically like the cords and tassels of some opulent tapestry [. . .] There, on the highest tier of this temple of gluttony [. . .] the altar display was crowned by a small, square fish tank [. . .] in which two goldfish swam in endless circles.[24]

The order in which these things are revealed is one of dastardly literary and moralizing craft: first the author employs all his gastropornic art in order to tempt the reader into sharing the salivating fascination of his hero; and only then, once we are helplessly dazed with imaginary tastes, does he hand down the editorializing judgement that this is a 'temple of gluttony', whose poignant crowning goldfish are, perhaps, meant to represent the pointless bestial circling of those interested in food above all else. The linkage of such gourmandist fascination with sex itself, meanwhile, is immediate: in the very next paragraph Florent gazes on 'a handsome woman' with 'glossy hair' and a 'swelling bosom', who 'had the fine skin and pinky-white complexion of those who spend their lives surrounded by fat and raw meat'. Florent's long visual appreciation of her figure is interrupted by Gavard informing him that she is his sister-in-law. So the erotic reverie is retrospectively perverted as incest, just as the food reverie is retrospectively denounced as gluttony.

A certain strand of foodism rejoices in the exotic: celebrating outlandish food becomes, instead of mainstream gastroporn, a kind of high-class fetish erotica. A great part of the appeal of *The Fat Duck Cookbook*'s recipes is the sheer novelty of apparently disgusting combinations (egg and bacon ice cream; olive and leather purée), as though we found ourselves suddenly transfixed by some outré flavour of bestial porn; yet we are simultaneously reassured that they are delicious and sanctioned by the latest science. (The horse really wants it.) One episode of the YouTube hit *Epic Meal Time*, meanwhile, features the construction of a foodist homage to the superbly revolting horror film *The Human Centipede*, in the shape of a 'TurBaconEpicCentipede', which consists of '10 roast piglets, stitched together nose to tail, each stuffed with a turkey, in turn stuffed with a duck, then a chicken, a Cornish hen and a quail, all of it dressed with strips of crisp bacon and a whole bunch of other stuff'. This is the deliberately disgusting 'comedy of excess', Jay Rayner notes, yet he worries that it will give his own blameless foodist 'greed' a 'bad name'.[25] That is, perhaps, the satirical point.

If one didn't know that it was published a half-century earlier, one might almost suspect some of the 'aphrodisiac' recipes in Norman Douglas's very funny cookbook, *Venus in the Kitchen*, to be satires of twenty-first-century cuisine and its insatiable desire for pseudoerotic shock value – for example, that for 'Hysterical Water': 'Take seeds of wild parsnip, betony, and roots of lovage, of each two ounces; roots of single peony four ounces; of mistletoe of the oak three ounces; myrrh a quarter of an ounce, and castor half an ounce. Beat all these together, and add to them a quarter of a pound of dried millipedes. Pour on these three quarts of mugwort water, and two quarts of brandy . . .'[26] One at first suspects satire in another recipe, that for 'Rôti sans pareil', until one checks Douglas's reference and finds that there really is an 1811 French cookbook that recommends stuffing seventeen birds, one into the other – this being 'the ne plus ultra of gastronomic ecstasy'.[27] (You put an olive inside a garden warbler inside an ortolan inside a lark inside a thrush inside a quail inside a lapwing inside a golden plover inside a partridge inside a woodcock inside a teal inside a guinea-fowl inside a duck inside a chicken inside a pheasant inside a goose inside a turkey inside a bustard.) For his part, Douglas warns, with gentle solemnity: 'It might be difficult to procure so varied an assortment of wild fowls anywhere at one and the same time.'[28]

Heston Blumenthal's perverse concepts (bee-egg omelettes!)[29] are only the latest exercises of a seam of jolly shock-foodism that reaches back past Carême's sugar castles to Roman times: 'a baked ham is cut to be served, only to have a flock of live birds fly out from a grotesquely pregnant dead belly. Diners sit at tables full to overflowing with delicate stews of udders and wombs [. . .] And Martial describes with particular relish "eiectitiae," a matrix from which the fetus has been removed before birth.'[30] Certainly the anti-foodist Roman moralists conflated their disgust at overeating with their disgust at sex, as in Horace's dour warning: 'The brothel and the greasy cookshop stir your longing.'[31] Plato's *Republic*, meanwhile, had already compared the desire for a wider variety of food than was necessary for 'fitness' with an immoderate sexual appetite, both tending to lead to the disaster of democracy.[32] Nonetheless, it is possible to denounce a pre-occupation with food without also disapproving of sex; indeed, it might be precisely because one approves so well of sex that one wants to resist the ambition to reduce it to an aspect of, or subsume it completely into, the mundane and consumerist practice of eating fancy victuals.

Bourdain has a theory as to why food in our mass-cultural times might have become 'the new porn': perhaps it offers 'a less dangerous alternative to the anonymous and unprotected shag of decades past'.[33] Or maybe it is just that, even in the accelerating pornification of everything in today's culture, it remains more respectable to display cookbooks than framed stills from sex movies in one's home. And the heavy-stomached, sluggish foodist, with all available blood diverted to his digestive organs, likely has rather more use for one than the other anyway.

6.

Fashion on a Fork

What's with all the hay? The hipster at the food rave had managed to incinerate a whole lamb's corpse with an out-of-control hay-based inferno, while Viajante smokes one starter over hay (it smells . . . countrysidey), and also sprinkles 'hay ash' over its butter (it tastes . . . ashy). Perhaps the mere invocation of hay invites us to daydream pleasantly about a beautiful, airy barn full of happy, resting animals, or an outdoor vista of haystacks dotted about rolling green hills. In any case, hay is suddenly everywhere in high foodism, one of the fashionable cooking accessories du jour. It might even be the new blowtorch. Perhaps, soon, cow dung will be the new hay.

Food, of course, has never been completely insulated from fashion and fad. There have been spectacular changes in what academics call 'food-ways' over the centuries: while the English have always adored fried bacon, for example, 500 years ago they sprinkled sugar on their oysters.[1] The 'restaurant' as we know it dates only from 1765, named for the restorative qualities of the broths served by the Parisian soupmaker Boulanger, and 'service à la Russe' (food brought in separate courses, on plates) is a relatively recent change from 'service à la Française', when everything was brought to the table together. In 1668, Pepys remarked with surprise on dining at a table 'with one little dish at a time upon it', but in 1862 it was still the fashion at dinner parties to serve everything at once, a practice that one dissenting writer attributed to 'the vanity of showing the plated side-dishes'.[2] (The first restaurant cook to serve his food 'already on the plate' was Jean-Baptiste Troisgros, who opened his joint in 1930.)[3]

But the pace of change today in what ingredient or dish or national cuisine is considered cutting edge seems neurotically accelerated, even by comparison with Escoffier's own lament, in 1907, for the impossibility of serving fresh cod or bass at his restaurant, because fashionable diners would turn up their noses: 'The culinary value of the fish has far less to do with the vogue the latter enjoys than the very often freakish whims of the public,' he noted sadly.[4] In modern times, high foodists positively celebrate the comparison with fashion: in 1984, *The Official Foodie Handbook* was already boasting that 'Couture has ceded the centre ground to food',[5] and Heston Blumenthal explains his refusal to water down his Fat Duck recipes for the ordinary cook by comparing his productions with 'haute couture' rather than high-street imitations.[6]

Fondue was all the rage in the 1970s; Marks & Spencer's prawn-mayonnaise sandwich kicked off the 1980s; Josh Homme's favoured sushi became mainstream in the 1990s along with 'wood-oven pizzas and grilled everything'.[7] Jenny Linford's close analysis of the cookbooks of Delia Smith shows the cook deftly keeping up with trends in new ingredients: in 1989 Delia was using the newly trendy filo pastry; in 1993 she introduced sun-dried tomatoes, and in 1995 Thai fish sauce.[8] By 1997, people had gone crazy for mushrooms, and everyone suddenly knew what a cep was. We can surely be happy that in our day olive oil is no longer sold exclusively in chemists and labelled 'for external use', as it was in the 1950s,[9] and that all kinds of other scrumptious things are now available. But the tempo of foodist faddism has become ridiculous, as represented by Sudi Pigott's celebration of its arbitrary rules: 'the Better Foodie is quietly smug about not buying, cooking or ordering any former gastro-must-eats beyond their Better Foodie use-by date [. . .] Hence, beetroot has been routed out [*sic*] by celeriac; and kohlrabi, pinky skinned chiogga is still acceptable [. . .] Cavolo nero has been superseded by ruby chard.'[10] (According to Pigott, an ingredient can even be 'directional', like a new style of jean or shoe.) By 2011, a pheasant-loving foodist lamented the fact that his favoured game bird was no longer fashionable, since 'Game snobs prefer grouse and woodcock'.[11]

In the same year, Britain went bread-and-cake mad, thanks to the success of a TV show called *The Great British Bake Off*:

baking's homely, rustic air perhaps provided some comfort in the tanking economy. Primrose Bakery's 'boutique bakery app' for smartphones, offering instructions for cupcakes, layer cakes, loaves, biscuits, and icings, became a surprise hit, topping the food-app charts in the US, Britain, Australia, and Canada.[12] Yet at the same time, frozen yoghurt – or, if you will, FroYo – was allegedly 'whisking the limelight away from coffee shops and juice bars', thanks to the arrival of a Californian yoghurt shop, Pinkberry, in the haut-bourgeois department store, Selfridges.[13] (At Viajante they grate frozen yoghurt over their ice cream.)

Foodist trends can now necessitate linguistic back-formations in order to identify something you could once take for granted. In summer 2011, the menu at a north London gastropub (itself a term that has now fallen from fashion: the *Good Food Guide* has announced that they will no longer use it)[14] featured a dish that included 'Hen's eggs'. This was confusing to me, until I realized that what they meant was simply 'eggs'. But people have presumably become so blasé about being offered the eggs of ostriches or dinosaurs that to say merely 'eggs' these days invites a perilous foodist uncertainty.

Naturally, there are fashions not only in ingredients but in styles of cooking. The so-called 'molecular gastronomy', first christened by Hervé This and the British physicist Nicholas Kurti in 1988[15] and subsequently practised by such cooks as Heston Blumenthal (though he disdains the term), Ferran

Adrià, and Nuno Mendes, was pronounced dead by This himself in 2009, because it was 'fashionable'.[16] This proposed instead his archly modernist 'culinary constructivism', which apparently means making weird-tasting three-dimensional chessboards out of black-and-white jelly.[17] But drizzles and foams are still going strong. In one episode of *The Trip*, the duo are served 'scallops in caper emulsion'.

BRYDON: I'm undecided on the froth.
COOGAN: It's part of the zeitgeist innit, the
culinary zeitgeist.[18]

In late 2011, meanwhile, the journalist Suzanne Moore, while protesting that she was not a 'food barbarian', exclaimed in disgust that she had been served 'scum' by Tom Aikens (its official title was 'Foam of Cauliflower').[19] My own lemony 'emulsion' (or so I think it was described) that was squirted next to the roasted celeriac at Viajante reminded me mainly of a lather of citrus-scented Gillette.

But the new new thing at the time of this writing is, apparently, 'neurogastronomy', a spectacular marriage of foodist high-culture aspiration with the parascientific trend of attaching the prefix neuro- to just about everything. According to an enjoyably sarcastic account by Frank Bruni, the New York 'neurogastronomist' cook Miguel Sánchez Romera 'favors squishy textures, kaleidoscopic mosaics of vegetable powders, and a wedding's worth of edible flowers', and describes his foodist discipline as one that 'embodies a holistic approach to food by means of a thoughtful study of the organoleptic properties of each ingredient'. 'Organoleptic,' Bruni explains patiently, means 'perceived by a sense organ'.[20] So Romera's philosophy means that he wants the food to look, smell, and taste nice, as well as presumably being pleasant to touch and making a mellifluous noise. Marinetti himself would approve.

There are trends, too, in serving styles: no self-respecting pork chop would currently be seen dead on anything other than a slate; several of the dishes at Viajante were served on warm or cool pottery 'stones'; and chips these days are, somewhat mystifyingly, served in 'beakers', both at high-end restaurants and chain bistros. And fashion rules the availability of culinary equipment for the amateur foodist: the Global brand of Japanese knives found its sales skyrocketing after Anthony Bourdain recommended them, and it is now possible in a grand department store to choose from a bewildering array of, say, mortar-and-pestle sets. (At John Lewis in London, I also saw, in a poignant sign of these singleton times, a tiny frying pan designed to fry exactly one egg, and a tiny griddle pan for cooking exactly one steak.) The blowtorch, meanwhile, seems to have been made fashionable by Marco Pierre White, who writes that when he opened Harvey's, 'we were skint, we couldn't even afford a grill. So we played around with a blowtorch for gratins and glazes, and it worked really well.'[21] Since then, one has needed a blowtorch even if one is lucky enough already to have a grill, because there is something so satisfyingly macho and torture-porn about using it. If, twenty years on, the blowtorch has lost some of its novelty value, the designers of kitchen gadgetry are always at work dreaming up something new. As of 2011, you can buy a food processor that also heats the ingredients, a 'Kenwood Cooking Chef' that, according to a print advertisement, allows you to 'make even the most challenging recipes quickly and easily'. The cost? A thousand pounds, give or take a fiver. Conspicuous consumption squared.

The modern fashionability of foodism in all its flavours shows fashion itself coming full circle. In 1862, the splenetic foodist author of *Dinners and Dinner Parties*, a rant about how women ought to learn to cook rather than being distracted by useless education, lamented the vanished golden age of a century before, when 'the art of cookery was fashionable among English girls and English wives [. . .] The art of making wine, pickling, and preserving, were the gentlewoman's morning amusements.'[22] And now they are again; not to mention the resurgence of interest in other skills that Christopher Driver worried, in 1983, were dying out: how to 'make bramble jelly or marmalade; skin a rabbit or pluck and draw a chicken; make a batter pudding; bake potatoes in the ashes of a bonfire; taste a farmhouse cheese made of unpasteurised milk; be offered cucumber sandwiches at teatime; find a pub selling scrumpy cider'.[23] It seems that modern foodists must even impose the same enthusiasm on innocent and defenceless members of their own household, or so report Josée Johnston and Shyon Baumann in *Foodies: Democracy and Distinction in the Gourmet Foodscape*, a fascinating sociological analysis of modern foodism: 'In the neighbourhood where we live, a food journalist recently reported that "foodie children" are the hot new accessory, and described overhearing parents proudly boasting that their children ate pig intestines at local Korean restaurants.'[24] One wonders how that compares with the Dawkinsite's view of inculcating religion into children as a kind of child abuse.

We might want seriously to defend the following of fashion in general, as well as the following of foodist fashion, as a defence strategy to insulate the individual against the onerous ubiquity of choice. This is the interesting stance taken, for example, by John Watters's analysis of the fashionability-as-psychosis of Patrick Bateman in Bret Easton Ellis's masterpiece, *American Psycho*. Bateman becomes enraged when a restaurant pizza does not conform to the rules on pizza of the food journalism he consumes and has memorized as law. 'No one wants the fucking *red snapper pizza!*' he cries. 'A pizza should be *yeasty* and slightly *bready* and have a *cheesy crust!* The crusts here are too fucking thin because the shithead chef who cooks here overbakes everything! The pizza is dried out and brittle!' Watters comments, sympathetically: 'The randomness, and choice, which comes from not following fashion is too awful to contemplate.'[25] But what modern foodist fashion in particular dictates at any one time is a relatively small variety of sanctioned ingredients, among each of which there is still a numbing array of choice, so that one is obliged to pick one out of a modern supermarket's twenty different varieties of olive oil. (The professor of food and health policy Martin Caraher observes: 'As food choice has increased a curious conundrum has occurred with people eating a narrower range of foods.')[26] When considering the purchase of a fashionable pair of jeans or bag, one still has to choose between various 'designer' and 'high-street' brands, but the foodist arguably has it worse. He experiences the downside of enslavement to fashion (having to follow the contingent whims of 'tastemakers'), with none of the upside: the blessed restriction of choice. (This might actually be commercially counterproductive for those seeking to profit from foodism: it has been shown that shoppers given the choice of twenty-odd varieties of jam are less likely to buy any jam at all than if they are offered a more manageable number of options – for instance only six.)[27] And foodist fashion-accessory children have it even worse again: they are given no choice about being forced to become choosy.

One must even now choose between several different kinds of goose fat in tubs available at the supermarket – that is, assuming one just has to have some goose fat in the first place, and if one is a foodist, one does. The existence of this new product is rather a beautiful example of foodist fashion: to eat a goose itself is not trendy, but to roast your potatoes in goose fat certainly is. One wouldn't dream nowadays of roasting potatoes in anything else. But what to do with the bloody goose? (You want the goose? You can't handle the goose.) Well, now you can buy the fat alone in plastic tubs: in this way, the messy, supererogatory bird (an inconvenient goose) has been magicked from the shopper's consciousness, leaving only the directional adiposity. One day, the scientists of animal flesh grown from cell cultures in a Petri dish without harm to actual animals (a project happily dubbed 'meat without feet') will no doubt also be able to grow us massive vats of goose fat, thus saving us (or food packagers) having to go to all the trouble of discarding the goose first.

7.

Consuming History

On a wooden chopping board in front of me is what looks like a mandarin, down to the perfect dimpling on the orange skin and the green stalk and leaf. But my probing knife offers no peel resistance (or 'fightback', as the cheesemakers' term of art has it); instead, the skin yields butterishly to reveal a homogeneously pale-brown interior, which is a delicious chicken-liver parfait. I am eating 'Meat Fruit', a dish already pronounced 'legendary' by the foodist cognoscenti,[1] at Heston Blumenthal's London restaurant, Dinner, aka Dinner by Heston Blumenthal. (Like Michael by Michael Kors, it's the more accessible, mainstream version of the brand.)

Here there is no liquid nitrogen, and diners are not forced to listen to sound effects over headphones in order to enhance their tasting experience. Instead, the menu consists of Heston's 'interpretation' of historical British food, and it carefully lists the 'Sources of origin' in cookbooks of centuries past. In this way my companion and I learn that her 'Rice and Flesh' starter – a pungent saffron risotto with soft bits of calf's tail floating in it – originates 'c.1390' in the earliest English cookbook, *The Forme of Cury*; and that her excellent 'Spiced pigeon' main course is from 1777's 'The Ladies' Assistant and Complete System of Cookery by Charlotte Mason'. (My own 'Meat fruit' is dated to 'c.13th–15th century'.) The main course I eat, the 'Hereford ribeye' steak – not a great steak, but cooked to a supernaturally even medium-rare – is allegedly from 'c.1830' since it is served with a 'mushroom ketchup' described around then, as well as with Blumenthal's famous 'Triple cooked chips' – which disappointingly (but as the name in a way warns) taste of old, congealed grease. I suspect Heston hasn't been able to stop himself from inserting a bit of the old molecular-gastronomy magic for the puddings, though: I have a confection involving ginger ice cream, chocolate, and raspberry which is at once one of the most confusing and delicious things I have ever eaten in my life.

Overall, Dinner serves a very decent meal in highly congenial surroundings: pleasantly free of performing waiters in period costume, say ruffs and tights, spouting cod-Elizabethan English to the accompaniment of lutenists, as might be thought appropriate by a cook intent at his other restaurant upon imposing a multisensory 'performance' upon his captive audience. And since I have been warned by a kindly waiter, apologizing for the lack of perfect edibility of the 'Meat Fruit', I don't have to pick a wax faux-stalk out of my teeth afterwards.

Dinner is but one example of how, just as fashion repeats itself – stay alive long enough and your old clothes will be in again, however momentarily – so foodism itself has lately entered a retro or revivalist phase in which, according to a quasi-scholarly procedure, it 'interprets' and consumes its own history. Certain foods already enabled a kind of backwards time-travel, or so argued Roland Barthes, noticing a 'historical theme' in 1960s French food advertising, and arguing that 'through his food the Frenchman experiences a certain national continuity'.[2] Perhaps this is now what foodists are attempting to provide to the discontinuous Anglo-Saxon. One episode of *Celebrity MasterChef* in 2011 saw the social historian Ruth Goodman cooking 'historical' dishes such as 'Bedfordshire Clangers' (suet puddings with meat at one end and jam at the other) and an 'Apple and Quince Pie' topped with cheesy custard. Grant Achatz's new Chicago restaurant, Next, opened in April 2011 by serving a 'Paris 1906' menu based on the recipes of Auguste Escoffier himself. In Britain in the same year, Clarissa Dickson-Wright, one of the 'Two Fat Ladies', published *A History of English Food*, and the publisher Penguin launched its 'Great Food' series, in which extracts from old cookbooks (Mrs Beeton, Gervase Markham, Eliza Acton) or miscellanies of passages about food by other writers (Pepys, Lamb) are republished in dinky paperback form. For an event in London's Foyle's bookshop in September 2011, the series editor Pen Vogler had not only prepared a talk but also baked several 'historical' cakes for the audience to taste. A Marchpain, cooked according to a 1615 recipe with marzipan and rosewater, tasted a bit like Turkish Delight; a 1747 caraway-and-sack cake was boozy; an 1845 ginger and treacle cake was powerfully oleaginous. The idea seemed to be hanging in the air over the young, Vuitton-toting audience that eating could be a more reliable, as well as easier, way to learn about the past than mere intellectual activity.

One could excitingly have it both ways, by composing a 'history' book that is really all about food. Cita Stelzer's 2011 *Dinner with Churchill* is arranged around eight diplomatic dinners during the Second World War and afterwards, complete with menus and seating plans, so that one may marvel at the great man putting away a fried sole wrapped in smoked salmon with scampi on top before proceeding to a main course of roast deer stuffed with foie gras and accompanied by truffle sauce. The book gamely attempts some food-based political analysis, but it is really a brilliantly conceived artefact that enables foodists to indulge their all-consuming gastromania even while notionally learning about something more intellectually nourishing. The example of Winston Churchill himself – who was, not to mince words, a fabulous glutton as well as a heroically prodigious boozer – must be particularly edifying to the modern foodist, who may be tempted to suppose that the great man's preternatural pluck and resolve can be attributed to all that caring-about-food rather than to the strength of character which the modern foodist himself, a slave to fashion and his own yawning gullet, so conspicuously lacks.

Heston's 'Meat Fruit' dish was actually invented, or if you will 'excavated' (one hears talk these days of 'food archaeologists', seriously), by one Marc Meltonville, the head of the 'Historic Kitchens' team at Britain's Historic Royal Palaces organization. He has also 'successfully produced a cockatrice, a Tudor specialty that joins the bottom of a pig and the head of a turkey. (You sew them together.)'[3] (No one knows why.) The main attraction at Hampton Court is now its 'Tudor Kitchens', where growling-stomached tourists can observe the preparation of old recipes, and participate in an Elizabethan-cookery workshop or 'Historic Cheese Tasting Session'. For the *New Yorker*, Lauren Collins visited Hampton Court and helped Meltonville, along with curator and historian Lucy Worsley, try to 'whip up the dinner that King George III ate on the evening of February 6, 1789', for no apparent reason.[4] The repast included some barley soup, partridges, and a spit-roasted leg of mutton. 'The partridges, heart-shaped and lustrous, sat atop a bed of spinach,' writes Collins (though, as we know by now, the partridges could not in fact sit on a bed, because they were dead). Worsley samples the partridge and squeals: 'I think they taste like rats!'[5]

Revivalism is a trend even in fast food, as I discovered by nomming a McDonald's '1955 Burger', which is advertised with nostalgic imagery of old-school American diners. The product is in its way a marvel of psychogastronomic engineering. It looks more like a 'proper' (*q.v.*) burger than the chain's normal anaemic 'patties', with a cosmetic chargrilled effect, and the first half-second of the flavour is pretty much 'proper burger', until the burger flavour abruptly vanishes to be replaced by the flavour of the bacon, the onions, and the 'smoky' barbeque sauce, at which point you realize that the 'burger flavour' was only ever a kind of chemical virtual-reality simulacrum. This weirdly fascinating journey of flavour-sublimation – from apparently real to ghostly simulation – keeps on happening with every bite of the burger, making the experience oddly satisfying, except to the stomach.

Curiously for a product ostensibly celebrating McDonald's founder Ray Kroc's first burger joint, the 1955 Burger did not launch in America but in Germany in 2010 (where it rapidly became that country's 'best-performing sandwich'),[6] whence it began a triumphal march across Europe into the UK. At the time of this writing it was still only 'under consideration' for launch in the US market. From the European TV commercials announcing the 1955 Burger – a Swedish spot features neon, finned shiny cars, and a sweet elderly man remembering the time he went to the first McDonald's 'restaurant' – it is evident that its function is primarily to sell the nostalgic image of a friendly, happy America to foreigners, before they try doing the same to Americans themselves. I would wager that in this way the McDonald's 1955 Burger achieved more for international goodwill towards America, enhancing that country's 'soft power' around the globe, than Barack Obama managed in the same period.

Foodist language, too, is contributing to foodism's retro revival. 'Heritage' produce is a term for breeds of tomato, apple, and so forth that were once in use in this country but which fell into desuetude in favour of the majority monoculture of a few high-yield varieties. The foodist who agitates for 'heritage' produce thus evinces nostalgia for a simpler, bucolic past, as well as a caring ecological concern for 'biodiversity' (of which more later), and handily also marks himself out as the kind of sophisticated person who can distinguish between flavours of cucumber. (The result is not always discernible, however, even to the professional palate. A.A. Gill writes caustically of one effort so labelled: 'A heritage tomato salad was a tomato salad made with tomatoes that desperately tried to live up to its £12 price tag.')[7] Perhaps it is in order to finesse the possible connotations in 'heritage' of boring tours through country houses and gardens that the alternative term 'heirloom' is sometimes used, though it is in a way even more ridiculous. (A piece of food that was passed down reverently through the generations would be at best a blackened, wizened husk or heap of collapsed rot.) But 'heirloom' does appeal to a fantasy of personal wealth in a way that 'heritage' does not, and is thus more seductively individualist. Paul Theroux has written a fabulously purple paean to 'heirloom tomatoes', advertising his own weirdly erotic connoisseurship: 'My preferred tomato is a fist-size Brandywine or a sooty, plumlike Black Ethiopian or a red, ribbed Conestoga [. . .] all these heirlooms are evenly deep-hued and luscious on the inside, as crimson and soft as mouth flesh.'[8] (Mouth flesh? Hello?)

Perhaps in eating a 'heritage' food, it is one's national heritage that one is imaginatively consuming and absorbing, becoming Disraeli and Churchill both. Of course, British food in particular has been a smorgasbord of immigrant cuisines at least since the Norman Conquest. That is the theme of Jamie Oliver's 2011 television series, *Jamie's Great Britain*, which is about 'our glorious food Britannia', but is really a cheerily explicit advert for immigration and multiculturalism. Oliver is always at pains to explain that what we might think of as 'British' food came from somewhere else: 'the whole concept of pies came from Egypt'; or: 'You take something quintessentially British like fish and chips – it's not English! It's Jewish.'[9] Whether he is lovably shucking oysters on a jetty or flirting with grannies in a street market, Oliver is mounting a (very admirable) campaign against racism through what is ostensibly a food programme, thus once again using foodism as a Trojan horse for his political projects, sweetening the bitter pill of philosophy with a cheeky Bloody Mary sauce. The project can even be read as an implicit denunciation of parallel political events: by the time the show aired, the British government's tabloid-pandering anti-immigration policy had made it impossible for restaurants to bring in chefs from India,

Bangladesh, and Pakistan, causing a 'crisis in the £3.2bn curry industry'.[10] The 'communities' secretary Eric Pickles then attempted risibly to assuage such worries by announcing a 'curry college' that would teach Brits to cook their own curry. This was trumpeted as part of the government's overarching 'integration strategy', though here the word 'integration' seems to have taken on the rather unusual sense of 'Sod off, we'll learn to do it ourselves', which we never could had it not been for innumerable earlier immigrants arriving with their delicious spice-wrangling skills. (Jamie's own anti-racism manages to coexist happily with his particular style of light-hearted celebratory nationalism, even if the latter is sometimes taken to adorably absurd lengths: in the literary incarnation of the multimedia product family that is *Jamie's Great Britain*, he writes: 'In 2012, we will host the Olympics for the first time since 1948, and the world will be looking at what we do, and how we do it. Thankfully, it's coming at a great moment for British food. I'm happy to say we've never been more ready or able to impress.'[11] So, er, during the Olympics, the world would be watching us . . . *cooking?*)

Jamie's Great Britain (in codex form) is also exemplary for the tension it reveals in the whole historic-food project. 'Ask any British person what their two favourite meals are and I reckon most people would say their mum's roast chicken and a curry,' Jamie begins, reasonably enough. But then he drops the concept-bomb: 'Well, welcome to empire roast chicken, a combination of both of those things.'[12] Did those things really need to be combined, or has the revivalist concept forced poor Jamie into such heterogeneous gimmickry? The burden of incessant novelty on the star cook who must produce a new book every year is onerous: as the critic David Sexton has noticed, Jamie's oeuvre is riddled, as it can't help but be, with tiny variations on pasta with tomato sauce, scallops and bacon, or indeed roast chicken: '"My perfect roast chicken" (*The Naked Chef*), "Fantastic roasted chicken" (*The Return of the Naked Chef*), "Roast Chicken with lemon and rosemary roast potatoes" (*Jamie's Dinners*), "Perfect Roast Chicken" (*Jamie's Ministry of Food*).'[13] But the novelty treadmill makes the culinary promise rather incoherent: as Oliver's voiceover introduces each TV episode, the story is that he is going on a journey to discover the nation's food 'so that I can cook up my own amazing new British classics'. The apparent oxymoron of 'new classics' pulls in two directions at once: if the cook dreams up something entirely new, it is not a classic (unless the arrogant claim is that it will become one in the future, which is not really Jamie's style, and I have my doubts about 'Empire Roast Chicken' for one); on the other hand, if he makes a 'classic', it is by definition not new.

Even if one were able to make a 200-year-old dish with exactly the same kinds of ingredients that were available at the time, it still wouldn't taste the same to us as it did to the people who ate it then, because we don't have the habit of eating the same kinds of things in general, or the cultural expectations. As Hampton Court's historic-kitchener Marc Meltonville admits: 'The big problem is that we're modern people who've grown up with refined sugars and refined proteins all of our lives [. . .] The Georgians were not as used to extremes. You've had your tongue burnt off by a Mexican chili, and you've been eating sugar cookies since you've been able to stand – if something's subtle, sweetened with rose petals, how are you going to be able to taste it?'[14] The implicit promise of historic foodism is that, through gustatory sensation, you can indulge in a kind of psychic time-travelling, knowing history in a (literally) visceral way. But the fact is that you can't taste the past, because you are not in the past. On the other hand, if we change or 'update' or 'reinterpret' a historical recipe, making it a 'new classic', it's no longer the real thing™.

8.

The Real Thing

The preference for what is designated 'heritage' or 'heirloom' bespeaks the foodist's anti-modern prejudice that what is currently eaten by the masses is a degraded industrial hybrid, and it is by guzzling our way back to the rural past that we can recover something like authenticity in our food. 'Authenticity' is one of the 'values' proclaimed by the 2011 'Lima Declaration' of mega-chefs headed by Ferran Adrià, and snobbish contests as to what constitutes the 'authentic' version of a particular recipe have long been an enjoyable pastime for foodists.

At one point in her memoir of life in France (before she returned to the US to become one of America's first TV cooks), Julia Child congratulates herself on having researched the 'real' recipe for bouillabaisse (in one cookbook), and thus considers that she has refuted a proud Marseillaise who insists that real Mediterranean folk would never add tomatoes, the Marseillaise having been silently cheered on by the reader who has no firm opinion on whether tomatoes should or should not be added to bouillabaisse but is heartened to see a Frenchwoman defending her 'heritage' from a stuck-up tourist. For Child, however, invocation of the tomato-including recipe from Reboul's *Cuisinier Provençal* decides the argument definitively in her favour – 'So there!' she writes, with a little victorious shriek – leaving her to reflect on the character flaws of the poor Frenchwoman. 'Such dogmatism, founded on ignorance,' Child sniffs, authentically. She does not neglect, either, to inform us that this anecdote generalizes to a permanent superiority: 'Because I had studied up on everything, I usually knew more about a dish than the French did.'[1] Child is making the bad mistake of supposing that a single true or 'authentic' version of any traditional dish cooked over generations by ordinary French folk could even exist, still less be definitively preserved, unchangeable on pain of charges of ignorance and rude condescension by Americans, in a book. She also demonstrates the general truth that, though the committed foodist may look askance at the increasingly popular phenomenon of 'competitive eating' in the US and Japan (scoff, say, fifty-nine hot dogs in ten minutes), all modern foodism is competitive eating as well, with exoticism or authenticity replacing sheer quantity as the criterion of victory. For fairness' sake it ought to be noted that, later in her memoir, Child also confesses to using a garlic press, which for others (including Anthony Bourdain) is itself the height of inauthentic bourgeois pretension.[2]

*

Another food fashion that plays on notions of authenticity is the 'pop-up', a commercialized and trendified version of what used to be called a 'supper club'. In 2009, declared the *Independent*, 'underground, "pop-up" restaurants in private homes' were 'the latest foodie fad to hit London'. In obeisance to the recent post-millennial fashions in asymmetrical warfighting, the intrepid foodist attending a 'pop-up' was pictured as indulging in 'guerrilla dining', like some sort of Che Guevara of the chitterling. Snacking thus was totally authentic: 'In many ways, pop-up restaurants are a return to real eating, when dining out was a social event worth dressing up for and getting excited about, and food was about fresh, seasonal ingredients cooked well but without gimmickry.'[3] Just imagine: if you have never been to a 'pop-up', you have never done any real eating.

The 'pop-up', then, is authentic, and also somehow 'street', remaining so even as it sneaks out of its 'underground' origins in private apartments and houses and becomes a fully fledged commercial destination, albeit at an allegedly temporary location. 'Londoners adore a gritty pop-up,' said that city's newspaper, the *Evening Standard*, in late 2011. It described a new one called The Big Red, a pizza restaurant run out of an old No. 30 bus, parked in Deptford. Its appeal, the writer admitted, had little to do with the actual food; instead prospective customers were meant to appreciate the Shoreditchers-slumming-it ambience: 'The project is beautifully designed in that shabby chic way – seaside decking, planters with basil, honeysuckle, lavender, arty chairs and tables, tea lights in glasses. There are two sprawling white sofas and single booths where you can flirt or work on the laptop.'[4] So the pretensions to grimy authenticity of the 'pop-up' and its customers were elegantly, if perhaps unintentionally, punctured. (If pop-up entrepreneurs really wanted to be as authentically 'street' as their admirers liked to portray them, they could always sell freshly cooked food from street carts, like the New York City traders who hawk delicious Korean or Vietnamese food.)

Paradoxically, even world-renowned star cooks can now have their own 'pop-ups', as with Thomas Keller's October 2011 residency at Harrods in London. 'Chefs such as Angela Hartnett and Tom Aikens forked out £250 a head (minus booze and service) for the hottest dining ticket of the year,' a newspaper enthused.[5] (That month, Keller appeared on the BBC's Saturday-morning TV cooking show, *Saturday Kitchen*. He seemed a thoroughly nice man, and even a little nervous, since he does not ordinarily cook on television; nonetheless, his principles would not allow him to approach the jokey guest challenge in the appropriate spirit. Asked to cook a three-egg omelette as quickly as possible for the show's regular competition, Keller recorded the slowest time of any guest ever, insisting with charm and humour – but an iron will – on the necessity of 'gentle cooking'.) For the December 2011 Taste of Christmas foodist festival in London, it was possible to book in advance a 'Jamie Oliver's Dining Ticket' for 'The Big Feastival Pop-up Restaurant' at the eye-watering price of

£75, allegedly in support of the Jamie Oliver Foundation, though the small print revealed that the Foundation would see only £2 of that. The famous cook's 'pop-up', in the end, is merely a cynical exercise in adding another variety of scarcity to the experience in order to render it the more desirable: to the topographic scarcity of a normal restaurant (there are only so many covers) is added the temporal scarcity of the pop-up: it will exist only for a specified time, so you'd better hurry. (It is in a way analogous to the increasing fashion in London for restaurants where you can't book: if you have had to stand outside in the cold for two hours before being allowed to eat a hamburger at Meat Liquor, you might be tricked into thinking it's the best hamburger you've ever tasted.) In its desire to make hay from mere temporariness, the pop-up is just a high-end analogue of the Cadbury's Creme Egg, a delectably ultra-gooey British confection once sold only at certain times of the year. And if it's now possible to use the term 'pop-uppers' to describe people 'who work in the food industry but don't want to open a permanent restaurant',[6] it might just be more straightforward, and look less desperately try-hard, to call them itinerant cooks.

It is the French who supply the term for another important sub-strand of foodist authenticism: *nostalgie de la boue*. Literally, that means nostalgia for mud; it denotes a desire to return to the supposedly filthy but somehow more honest habits of the labouring class. It seems to have been Renaissance *nostalgie de la boue* that was responsible for the rediscovery and incorporation into high-class European cuisine of dairy products, previously despised as stuff the poor had to eat because they had nothing else. The strain of nostalgic pastoralism during the Enlightenment, meanwhile, saw French aristocrats building 'mock dairies in their gardens', which were thankfully free from 'cows and heaps of dung'.[7]

Certain flavours of snobbish nostalgia have long been evident in foodist writing, too: for example, Elizabeth David's condescendingly approving description of a 'primitive Cretan taverna',[8] or Sophie Dahl's 'Peasant soup'.[9] In modern foodism, the summit of *nostalgie de la boue* is to 'rediscover' the common man's food, to celebrate it, and subsequently re-elaborate it, so that the common man still can't afford to eat it. Fergus Henderson was a pioneer in making haute cuisine from the tripe and organs that used to be all the working classes could afford to eat. ('Cold Lamb's Brains on Toast': 'This is a dish for those who particularly enjoy the texture of brain.')[10] Thomas Keller's *French Laundry Cookbook*, meanwhile, contains many little jokes on working-class American food: for example, his 'Chips and dip': 'an American favorite, which we make a little more elegant by adding truffle to the chips and to the crème fraîche dip',[11] or his 'Chesapeake Bay Soft-shell Crab "Sandwich"': 'This is not really a sandwich, of course, but the dish was inspired by my love of traditional soft-shell crab sandwiches heaped with tomatoes and tartar sauce,' he writes fondly, before explaining how he arranges the dish. First the sauce goes on the plate, then 'On top of the sauce, I put a crouton, then the crab, trimmed down to just its body and claws, then tomato confit, arugula, and fried capers.'[12] The end result, in the photograph, looks like a taller and thinner version of Brueghel's *Tower of Babel*. After much study and three-dimensional mental manipulation (a faculty honed by years of playing videogames), I still cannot imagine how one is supposed to eat this '"sandwich"', unless it is possible to get the whole contraption in one's mouth in one go. Another smirking nod to the proles comes in Keller's version of '"Fish and chips"' (Keller's own scare quotes again), which is really 'Red Mullet with a Palette d'Ail Doux and Garlic Chips'.[13] (The 'chips' are what the British call crisps.) The dish consists of bits of fish stacked one atop another, in an apparent effort to freeze that moment in a game of Jenga just before the tower of wooden blocks collapses. Such culinary jokes about the working man's food were already parodied in the BBC comedy *Posh Nosh* – where, for instance, 'Builder's fish and chips' is reinvented as 'Architect's fish and chips'[14] – but high foodism, like the news media, is impressively immune to parody.

A condescending admiration for the humble foodmaker is present, too, in the fashion for 'artisanal' versions of low-class dishes: as Anthony Bourdain observes, in New York City the 'artisanal' pizza is edging out the 'utility slice'.[15] The recent rise of the word 'kitchen' – a gastropub becomes a 'bar and kitchen' – also plays to this kind of inverted snobbery, the utilitarian and democratic associations of 'kitchen' belying the fact that some 'kitchens' are still aimed squarely at the relatively wealthy. In September 2011, London saw the opening of Gordon Ramsay's Bread Street Kitchen, which was not a grain-focused, solids-based version of a soup kitchen, but a restaurant where starters were over £10 and main courses over £20: it was 'aimed squarely at the mid-market, City workers on "£40,000 or £50,000"'.[16] (And it served its chips in a 'beaker'.)

Eating an expensive or toy-like version of the working man's food is, like seizing on new ingredients, just another way of staying ahead of what the masses are eating. If the aspirational foodist nonetheless wants to eat ordinary food, he is reassured if it comes described as a 'gourmet' version, as in the Gourmet Burger Kitchen chain, 'gourmet popcorn', or even 'gourmet salt' (which, like all other salt, is mainly sodium chloride, just free of anti-caking additives).[17] You can even drink 'gourmet sodas' at high-end foodist destination restaurants. (In Harvey Levenstein's excellent social history of American food, *Paradox of Plenty*, he notes that there had previously been a mini-boom in 'gourmet' products in America in the late 1950s, when General Foods created a 'Gourmet Foods Division'.)[18] The consumer of a 'gourmet'-branded food product thus has it happily both ways, enjoying the thrill of slumming it with the common scoffers while being told that he is nonetheless a cut above in his gustatory discrimination. Everywhere, indeed, food is inextricably bound up with socioeconomic class.

David Sexton has argued that Britain in particular has a 'disintegrated, class-ridden food culture',[19] but the use of food to demarcate and signal social status is age-old and globally ubiquitous, as the social anthropologist Jack Goody shows in his study *Cooking, Cuisine, and Class*. Aristocrats in France have never eaten the same food as the poor; nor did they in Egypt 6,000 years ago, when the peasantry ate 'dates, vegetables and occasionally fish' while the ruling class dined from 'elaborate tables'; or in Mesopotamia three millennia ago, when the poor ate pickled fish and beef was for the rich.[20] The Romans, worried about the decadent feasting of the rich, passed sumptuary laws, and in ancient Indian texts 'the caste system itself is partly defined in terms of the type of food a man is allowed to eat', while medieval Arab cookbooks mandate exotic and expensive ingredients, simple foodstuffs being 'despised as pertaining to the lower orders'.[21] Joanna Blythman, author of *Bad Food Britain*, complains that 'good food in Britain has come to be considered posh', apparently under the impression that this has happened more recently than (at least) the Norman Conquest, and the subsequent introduction of French to describe the dinners of the aristocracy.[22] (It is true that the French who stayed in France have long regarded British food as all but inedible, as exemplified by the magnificent *de haut en bas* witticism of Jean Cocteau: '*A partir de 1940, les Anglais sont restés seuls . . . avec leur cuisine.*')[23]

Jon Henley, surveying British eating habits for the *Guardian*, makes a broad claim:

> Food has become, more than ever, one of the main indicators of social and class distinction in our society. If we're well off, we're more likely to eat well: fresh, unprocessed, nutritious, locally produced, bought at a farmers' market or small independent supplier. (We may also, of course, choose not to eat well, for reasons of time and convenience.) If we're not well off, we're more likely to eat badly: preserved, processed, high in sugar, fat and starch, mass-produced, bought from a convenience store or deep-discounter. (We may also, of course, be poor yet choose to make eating well our top priority.)[24]

This is as true in France or America as it is in Britain; but there is also a class distinction operative in how Henley draws his class distinction: what counts as eating 'well' or 'badly' depends on a lot of fashionable assumptions ('locally', 'processed', on both of which more later) that have been different in the past and might be different in the future. As Adam Gopnik points out, to eat well was once to eat foods that were out of season;[25] white bread used to be for the rich but now – 'paradoxically', as Roland Barthes noticed already fifty years ago – it is brown bread that is the 'sign of refinement'.[26] So a topical middle-class foodist's definition of eating 'well' is used to wring one's hands over how 'badly' the less fortunate are eating.

The modern Anglosphere is not unique, then, in the fact that eating habits are different between different socioeconomic classes (though Britain does, proudly, munch more than half of all the crisps eaten in Europe);[27] nor is it unique in its devotion to media foodism. Though Britain might lead the world in at least this respect (the BBC's *MasterChef* is hugely popular in twenty-nine countries), most nations have their home-grown food-based media too. In France there is the ubiquitous and super-smiley TV demonstrator and cookbook-writer Carinne Teyssandier, and the Hollywoodesque Julie Andrieu, currently presenter of three different food shows and author most recently of a book of 200 chocolate recipes.[28] Germany has a chummy chefs' roundtable called *Lanz Kocht!* and a hugely popular *Come Dine with Me* equivalent entitled *Das Perfekte Dinner* (*The Perfect Dinner*); and Sweden suffered a shortage of butter in 2011 after its celebrity chef Leila Lindholm, known for her 'cleavage-enhancing blouses', recommended Swedes embrace dairy rather than low-fat spreads. (Norway in turn ran out of butter later that year after a media-induced orthorexic craze for high-fat diets.)[29]

According to an intriguing recent study on food and class in modern-day America, the use of food to indicate status is prevalent even among those who cannot afford to indulge in refined conspicuous foodism, or who find it difficult actually to get hold of reasonably healthy food at all. (Large supermarkets where one might buy vegetables at reasonable prices do not open in deprived inner-city areas, creating what are known as 'food deserts' in the US.) The study authors surmise that the ordering of 'super-sized' portions in fast-food restaurants is not an issue of hunger or greed, but a way of compensating for a chronic lack of social status, because within the microsociety of the fast-food joint itself, the larger portion is perceived to reflect higher status. This is unfortunately counterproductive, the authors note, because it leads easily to obesity, which itself carries extra social stigma.[30] The *New York Times* columnist Frank Bruni, meanwhile, noted a 'class-inflected hypocrisy in the food world' after a public spat between Paula Deen, the celebrity 'down-home' cook specializing in fatty, Southern cooking, and Anthony Bourdain, who criticized her for telling 'an already obese nation' to eat more of the food that is 'killing' it. Yet, as Bruni wrote: 'When Deen fries a chicken, many of us balk. When the Manhattan chefs David Chang or Andrew Carmellini do, we grovel for reservations and swoon over the homey exhilaration of it all.'[31] Sometimes the only way to be sure of one's class distinction is just to pay a lot more for what amounts to the same thing, but has the extra psychic cachet of authenticity.

9.

Back to Nature

The best guarantor of food's authenticity is Nature herself. What is 'natural' is ipso facto maximally authentic, and so worthy of our respect. Indeed foodists regularly invoke, as one of their own cardinal virtues, 'respect for the ingredient'. How much 'respect' it can show to a blameless carrot (and foodists do claim to respect even vegetables) to rip it from the soil (thus killing it), then chop it, boil it, masticate it, and introduce it to the acids and bacteria of the human digestive tract is a nice question; let alone that of just how much 'respect' one shows a cow or pig by slaughtering it. On one episode of *MasterChef: The Professionals* in 2011, contestants had to prepare a wood pigeon to make it ready for roasting. Pleased with one man's job, Monica Galetti commented: 'He treated that pigeon with the respect it deserved.' The exact amount of respect it deserved, apparently, was to have its wings and head cut off with scissors, its feathers and entrails pulled out, and its stumps trussed to its torso. In just the same way, one can use the phrase 'with all due respect' as refined sarcasm to mean 'with just that amount of respect I consider you deserve: in other words, none'.

The idea that dismembering, heating, and chewing other organisms shows 'respect' for them seems to imply a very convenient teleology: that these things are all somehow destined for our stomachs, so that becoming obsessed about helping them into ourselves is the righteous way for us to contribute to the gradual Hegelian coming-to-know-itself of the world-gullet. Moreover, if a mushroom or a partridge actually desires to be eaten, it would be positively rude of us not to. The foodist, I suppose, does not quite believe that the life forms he consumes are like the cows in Douglas Adams's *Restaurant at the End of the Universe*, which walk up to diners' tables and happily chat about which bits of them are tastiest before ambling off to be killed and cooked. (Though higher-end steak joints such as the Gaucho Grill in London do now bring round examples of the raw cuts on a 'meat board'; and A.A. Gill describes sardonically another restaurant where the waiter 'intimates the last meals of the condemned. This one ate corn, this one grass, this one had beer and a massage'.)[1] Nor, I suppose, does the foodist quite share the notion of the eighteenth-century Scottish philosopher Thomas Reid, that vegetables have immaterial souls. Nor, again, do most foodists follow the strict version of Jainism according to which root vegetables such as potatoes and onions are eschewed because the whole plant would be killed. But then the foodist's avowal of 'respect' for what he is eating looks all the more like sanctimonious self-advertisement.

Thomas Keller, the foodists' foodist and cooks' cook, is very respectful. 'Another source of pleasure in cooking is respect for the food,' he avers. 'Respect for food is a respect for life.'[2] (Excluding, presumably, the life, of tuber or turtle, that has been taken for your incipient oral pleasure.) Anthony Bourdain, too, has the deepest respect for Keller's level of respect, writing dreamily of life backstage at the French Laundry: 'You haven't seen how he handles fish, gently laying it down on the board and caressing it, approaching it warily, respectfully, as if communicating with an old friend.'[3] Luckily, in the *French Laundry Cookbook*, a single moment of Keller's warily respectful handling of fish has been photographically immortalized: there he is in the restaurant kitchen, a kind of fish whisperer, holding his palms horizontally above a fish on a slab as though about to give it a revivifying qi massage. (He also, touchingly, stores his fish in 'the swimming position', though they will never swim again.)

When Bourdain dines at Fergus Henderson's London restaurant, meanwhile, Henderson himself comes over to eulogize the porky tail, saying: 'This was a very noble pig.'[4] If it really was such a 'noble' pig, one can't help asking, why wasn't it left alive, not to suggest installed in ermine robes as a life peer? Henderson himself, in the book that announced his millennial tripeist philosophy, explains: '"Nose to Tail Eating" means it would be disingenuous to the animal not to make the most of the whole beast.'[5] We can certainly approve of the 'waste not, want not' principle; yet a dead animal itself is surely past caring whether anyone is 'disingenuous' to it or not. Henderson's world turns out after all to be surprisingly close to that of the Restaurant at the End of the Universe. The food might be dead, but it still has opinions on how we should best eat it: 'The quail wants plenty of cooking'; stiff mayonnaise 'does not make a friendly partner for your crab'.[6] Such amiable, anthropomorphizing sentiments are in one way just pleasurable artefacts of Henderson's style, but one notices that they do all point one way – towards the denial of death and annihilation.

I am not suggesting that foodists should give up eating plants and animals if they don't want to. I eat meat, but I don't claim that my eating animals is a way of showing 'respect' for them. To do so is to exhibit just as much denial about what is involved as is supposedly exhibited (or so we are told by smug foodists) by the great unwashed masses who consume factory-farmed animal products. The foodist muncher's solemn invocation of his own 'respect' for what he is in the process of destroying looks dangerously like just another way of trying to sanctify his own guttishness, or (to modify one of George W. Bush's more memorable soundbites) to put lipstick on that very noble pig.

It is but a short step from 'respect' for the vegetable or animal to respect for the soil itself, which nurtures and nourishes us; indeed, according to the burbling finale of

Michael Pollan's *In Defence of Food*, it is only by cooking fresh food in your own kitchen that you know this food 'is no mere *thing* but a web of relationships among a great many living beings [e.g. plants, farmers, cooks], each of them dependent on the other, and all of them ultimately rooted in soil and nourished by sunlight'.[7] You might protest that you, for one, are not actually rooted in soil, and even walk about a bit to prove it, but this soil veneration, in which the most sublime possible state is apparently to resemble a vegetable, rooted and unmoving in the dappled sunshine, is entirely typical of a certain lineage of foodist rhetoric. Just as with Pol Pot's 'back to earth' movement, or the happy collectivized farm labourers of Soviet realism, the modern foodist lover of 'soil' evinces a kind of rustic primitivism, according to which eating is the best way to commune with Mother Nature, or perhaps the Fatherland.

Soil is hardly unimportant for the quality and amount of food that can be grown in it, and it is a proper subject of study for agricultural science; but foodist soil-worshippers are rarely satisfied with mere science. In their view, soil, like food, is somehow more than the sum of its parts. Hence the foodist's mystical attraction to the concept, imported from French winemaking, of *terroir*, for which 'foodie' Sudi Pigott announces her deepest 'respect'.[8] *Terroir* (originally French for 'land' or 'territory') was in nineteenth-century English used to describe an especially 'earthy' taste in wine or brandy; later it came to encompass all the particular (and often presumptively good) qualities of soil and climate in the region of production.[9] The hard-to-quantify variability of flavour owed to *terroir* is the basis of the *Appellation d'origine contrôlée* (AOC) system of wine-labelling in France, according to which you can call something a Bordeaux only if it was actually made there; not coincidentally, that also serves to protect French winemakers against grape-centric New World upstarts. AOC protection is also given in France to many cheeses, to Puy lentils (from Le Puy-en-Velay in the upper Loire) and to the world's most delicious chickens (from Bresse). In foodist and oenophile usage both, the implication is that the character (not to say spirit) of a place is gustatorily perceptible in its products, thus furnishing the eater with a special connection to the earth and flattering his own discriminatory powers. Naturally, soils in different regions have different compositions, which will influence to some extent the taste of the solid foodstuffs grown in them. But to what extent? Hervé This cites a study that compared the same variety of strawberry grown in different regions with different varieties grown in the same region. The study concluded: 'for taste, the variety is more important than the place of production'.[10] *Terroir* has some effect on the food (how could it not?), but perhaps not as much as its fetishists would wish.

People who love the loam, the hungry who honour the humus, seem to be more likely in general to think all kinds of other dubious things about food. Craig Sams of the Soil Association, for example, tells Jamie Oliver biographer Gilly

Smith that Chinese or Indian meals become 'imprinted' on our very DNA, and so do other things: 'We know that junk is imprinted on our DNA, too [. . .] Every time you drink a coffee or take ecstasy, or eat beef, it changes you and becomes part of your heredity.'[11] We might pause to ask why coffee, that miracle bean, is considered 'junk', and note the plausible argument of the biochemist Vincent Marks that there is no such thing as 'junk' food at all: 'To label a food as "junk" is just another way of saying "I disapprove of it". There are bad diets – that is bad mixtures and quantities of food – but there are no "bad foods" except those that have become bad through contamination or deterioration.'[12] Craig Sams's junk-genetics story has an initially puzzling flavour of crude Lamarckianism, supposing that acquired characteristics will necessarily be inherited, yet some recent research does seem to indicate that brain changes in rats fed 'fatty and sugary' food can be passed to their offspring, making the pups more liable to obesity and 'addictive-like behaviours'.[13] It hardly matters whether that turns out also to be true for humans, though, since Sams's theory is most significant rhetorically, for its marvellously subtle form of moral blackmail: to eat 'junk' is bad not only for you, he warns, but also for your as-yet-unborn children, who will inherit your disgustingly screwed-up beefy genome.

But then the foodist who venerates nature and the soil will despise 'processed' food of any kind, and always has. (Writing about such rhetoric in 1930s America, Harvey

Levenstein comments drily: 'To decry the processing of foods and proclaim the superiority of the "natural" represents an age-old current in America.')[14] Yet unless you eschew cooking completely and eat nothing but raw food (as some nincompoops actually do), you can hardly help processing what you eat: the transformations consequent on simply frying a slab of meat are extremely complex chemically. The food of the past was rarely all that pure and 'natural' anyway: in the nineteenth century, coffee was mixed with manure to give it a nice colour, and flour was mixed with plaster; and the advent of 'processing' was explicitly a way to combat this menace.[15] In Britain, the new 'processed' foods such as Hovis bread represented progress in safety as well as convenience, offering a certain reliability (symbolized by a system of royal patronage) to foods that had too often been adulterated and dangerous; they even contributed to the creation of a 'national cuisine'.[16]

The Soil Association, of course, is one of the founding institutions of 'organic' farming, itself long promoted as being based on 'respect for the soil'.[17] It might seem unfair to dwell on the fact that the Soil Association (which counts among its modern supporters the Prince of Wales, Sting, and Gwyneth Paltrow) was co-founded in 1945 by Jorian Jenks, a former member of the British Union of Fascists and chum of Oswald Mosley. But that may be a reflection of where concerns with purity and health of land, food, and body can lead. As one analysis of the 'organo-fascists' and back-to-the-landers of the 1940s in Britain puts it: 'organicist farmers in the "epoch of fascism" reviled mainstream farming methods for "killing the soil" on which all life depends, and for killing *British* soil in particular, for this especially fertile soil nurtured the now-threatened racial characteristics of the British'.[18]

The agricultural sense of 'organic' had itself been invented in 1940 by Walter James, fourth Baron Northbourne, an Olympic oarsman, agriculturalist, and devotee of the esoteric (not to say bullshit) 'spiritual science' promulgated by Rudolf Steiner.[19] Northbourne published a book entitled *Look to the Land*, in which he cooked up the phrase 'organic farming' to encapsulate his view of 'the farm as an organism' (a sort of microcosmic Gaia theory), and contrasted it with what he called 'chemical farming'. Of course, any 'organic' farm is also stuffed to the brim with chemicals. Chemicals are all there is. (Notes kitchen-science guru Harold McGee: 'Like everything on earth, foods are mixtures of different chemicals.')[20]

Many modern 'organic' practices are, let us agree, basically sensible. The modern Soil Association talks on its website of 'organic animals', as though most of us eat robotic animals, but the idea of pumping less in the way of antibiotics and growth hormones into the beasts we are going to eat, as well as giving them a comfortable existence (the appellation 'free range' is not always reliable in this respect), is a fine idea, as is the attempt to reduce the pollution engendered by the heavy use of some pesticides and fertilizers. But not all 'organic' practices are as clean and wholesome as their proponents would have us believe. For example, 'organic' farming certification in the UK allows the use of some pesticides, including the 'organic insecticide rotenone', which 'is highly neurotoxic to humans'.[21] The Soil Association pleads in its defence that rotenone is 'of natural origin'.[22] Great white sharks, death cap mushrooms, and the venom of the black widow spider are also of natural origin, but you wouldn't necessarily want them sprinkled on your food. And 'organic' foods can prove more dangerous than their industrially grown counterparts: 'organic' celery, for example, contains more 'natural' toxins than celery treated with pesticides, because the pesticides reduce the natural-selection pressure on the celery to defend itself with those same toxins from being eaten by insects.[23]

The naïve (or cynical) appeal to the idea that what is 'natural' must always be better is decidedly misanthropic, demoting human ingenuity and science in favour of the quasi-divine care offered us by a supposedly benign nature, and so is at one with the overall climate of humanity-hating Luddism that governs much catastrophist ecological thinking. (It does not follow from the fact that global warming is happening that we ought to dismantle industrial civilization; compare, too, the almost sexual relish with which 'peak oil' theorists forecast the world's collapse.) Bolivia's 2011 Law of the Rights of Mother Earth goes so far as to enshrine in that country's constitution the principle of granting 'nature' certain 'rights': for example, a right to life, and a right to freedom from genetic alteration. Of course, one cannot exactly enforce the latter right against the impersonal forces of genetic drift and natural selection, and it does not seem to be the case that all of 'nature' is to be treated as having the same value, since that would necessitate, among other things, the banning of antibiotics or mosquito countermeasures.[24] In this context of globally resurgent warm'n'fuzzy nature-worship, it is refreshing when Hervé This, almost alone among foodist intellectuals, insists that nature is 'bad for you' ('A nutmeg berry ground into powder can kill a person'), and that cooking is an artificial intervention meant to save us from it.[25]

There is no settled evidence that 'organic' foods are healthier, so the Soil Association, along with supermarkets redistributing its propaganda bulletpoints, has been regularly told by the Advertising Standards Authority to withdraw such claims.[26] Instead, 'organic' PR now focuses on claims about animal welfare and environmental 'sustainability', and promotes a terror of 'GM' food as hubristic interference with nature.

Many scientists, on the other hand, believe that genetically engineering more robust high-yield crops is the best way to ensure that we can feed an increasing global population. Antipathy to GM crops, or 'Frankenfoods', tends to be broad-brush and emotive, rehearsing the billions in profit-dollars made by Monsanto in order to feed a kneejerk anti-corporate prejudice. But 'Flood-tolerant rice, drought-tolerant sweet potatoes, salt-tolerant cassava, and high-yield millet [. . .] have the potential to feed more people — mostly poor people — with less land expansion and reduced pesticide application,' observes James E. McWilliams.[27] Critics evoke, among other worries, a 'threat to biodiversity from possible crossing between GM and non GM crops in the field'.[28] Biodiversity is certainly a great rhetorical virtue in our age; but the best way to maximize biodiversity might be to farm as little land as possible, using the highest-yield crops we can design. Gaia theorist James Lovelock himself has recommended intensive farming on limited land, just in order to prevent agricultural encroachment on virgin territory (like rainforest) where biodiversity is at its maximum.[29] And even 'biodiversity' can hardly be an absolute good in itself. The elimination of smallpox in the wild, forestalling enormous future human suffering, was a deliberate reduction in biodiversity. It would by contrast be an increase in biodiversity, though not obviously a cause for celebration, if some terrorist biologist introduced into the wild hundreds of newly engineered species of biting insects and poisonous moulds.

The emotive aspect of 'organic' publicity, in the absence of any right to make certain empirically unverified claims about the food, is perfectly exemplified in a poster that I caught sight of, and then stood before in trancelike admiration, in the window of a London branch of the pricey-produce shop Planet Organic. The image shows a smiling, rather plump man, perhaps in his late thirties, wearing a decorator's overalls and holding a paint-roller, sitting down next to a table on which is a cup of tea. He is smiling in satisfaction at the camera, while the text, designed to look hand-drawn by a thick black felt-tip pen, allows us into his innermost thoughts: 'I like organic because it feels right for my family.'

Note again the undertone of blackmail here, as with Craig Sams's zany theory of the heritability of coffee-induced DNA adulteration: not to buy organic would be a betrayal not only of yourself but of your loved ones. What is added to the mix by this poster is the implication that the choice to shop at Planet Organic, where no celery stalk or broccoli spear is deemed too obscenely expensive, should be made entirely on emotion. Indeed, the astronomic cost of 'organic' food (it can make a weekly shop more than twice as expensive)[30] is deftly obfuscated by choosing as the organic-loving hero of the advertisement a character who seemingly makes a living painting ceilings rather than shorting stocks. Even more interestingly, next to the man's cup of tea on the dust-sheeted table is what seems to be a pouch of rolling tobacco, thus subtly rebutting the stereotype of organic-buyers as orthorexic wellness freaks. So, look, you don't have to be rich, posh, or smugly healthy in order to buy organic food! You just have to care about your family! And if you don't buy organic food, you must hate your family! Usefully, this poster lays bare the entire promotional strategy of 'organics' in general: don't stop to think, just go with what 'feels' right and good. It remains to be seen whether this anti-rational tactic will help to reverse the downward trend of organic sales: by the end of 2011 in Britain, they had fallen by 23 per cent from their peak in 2008.[31]

The 'organic' movement may now have a stranglehold on 'green' talk in agricultural issues, but the development in the 1950s and 1960s of new farming techniques, crop hybridization, and synthetic fertilizers and pesticides was itself termed a 'green revolution': it vastly increased the amount of food that could be produced on any given area of land. Norman Borlaug, the American specialist in high-yield agriculture who was central to these developments, won the Nobel Peace Prize in 1970 for his role in eliminating the food shortages of India and Pakistan over the previous decade. Today he is scathing about Western eco-organicists who wish to deny the tools of industrial agriculture to the less fortunate: 'If they lived just one month amid the misery of the developing world, as I have for fifty years, they'd be crying out for tractors and fertilizer and irrigation canals and be outraged that fashionable elitists back home were trying to deny them these things.'[32] Since then, in the teeth of opposition from Greenpeace and other eco-bodies, the Bill and Melinda Gates Foundation has given $100 million to found the Alliance for a Green Revolution in Africa, 'to fund the research and production of drought-tolerant crops'.[33]

The excesses of the first 'green revolution', as publicized in Rachel Carson's *Silent Spring* (which coincided with the first 'organic' boom in late-1960s America), were indeed dangerous and the subject of proper outrage. (There followed, in the mid-1970s, a boom in the commercial rhetoric of 'natural' foods – 'natural potato chips, beer, deodorant, and even dog food with "natural beef flavor"'[34] – which continues to this day.) But the modern organicist's dream of reverting worldwide to the less productive farming methods that obtained before the mid-twentieth century will require, absent the mass conversion of billions to vegetarianism, and perhaps even then (no livestock, no 'organic' fertilizer, as Borlaug points out), far more of the planet's surface to be devoted to agriculture. And it is in regard to this utopian prospect, of re-rusticizing America and the world to constitute an endless series of 'small farms' as far as the eye can see – a world in which the poor, according to the American organic ideologue Alice Waters, will be expected to feast on 'heirloom' turnips and cabbages – that Anthony Bourdain repeatedly poses the devastatingly pertinent question: 'Who will work these fields?'[35]

Organicists who want to turn back the clock might do well to consult Upton Sinclair's *The Jungle*, which was not only a seminal text in its revelation of brutal and disgusting meat-production practices of the early twentieth century, but also predicted (in 1906) the invention of the washing machine.[36] During his peroration, the erudite and perhaps half-mad Swede Dr Schliemann laments:

> our present agonizing system of independent small farming – a stunted, haggard, ignorant man, mated with

a yellow, lean, and sad-eyed drudge, and toiling from four o'clock in the morning until nine at night, working the children as soon as they are able to walk, scratching the soil with his primitive tools, and shut out from all knowledge and hope, from all the benefits of science and invention, and all the joys of the spirit – held to a bare existence by competition in labour, and boasting of his freedom because he is too blind to see his chains![37]

It's hard to know quite how seriously the reader was meant to take this pungent mélange of sympathy and contempt, but it does seem a nice historical irony that what Schliemann described as a nightmare at the beginning of the twentieth century is now presented as the eco-friendly foodist utopia for the twenty-first.

Organicism likes to think of itself as 'planet-friendly' (a term from the Soil Association's website), and insists that it is the one truly 'sustainable' form of agriculture. But the term 'sustainable' very often glosses over the crucial questions: sustainable for whom, or for what, and on what set of evidence-based or emotionally apocalyptic assumptions? It's a strange set of ethical priorities, at least, that values an unrequitable 'friendship' with a massive hunk of rock floating in space over solidarity with one's fellow human beings. Yet organicists have long implied just that choice. In a 1969 article from the legendary eco-hippy-tech bible the *Whole Earth Catalog*, for example, one finds the following credo: 'I believe that organic gardeners are in the forefront of a serious effort to save the world by changing man's orientation to it, to move away from the collective, centrist, superindustrial state, toward a simpler, realer one-to-one relationship with the earth itself.[38] That's clear enough. Screw the 'collective'; screw everyone else; this is all about your own private feel-good 'relationship with the earth', a properly anti-social solipsism à deux, in which one partner isn't even a conscious being. The foodist who promulgates 'organic' absolutism, in short, wants masses of unnamed others to do the back-breaking labour of pre-industrial agriculture on his behalf, just so that he can feel better about his intimate liaison with the planet.

10.

Eating to Utopia

A devotion to 'organics' is just one example of the most ambitious way that the modern foodist insulates himself from potential charges of mere hedonistic crapulosity, which is to insist that his fixation on chow is not just self-indulgence but a way of changing the world for the better. Choosing the right food is taken to be an ethical act. To shop for dinner is thus to perform one's moral superiority. '"Eat your view!" is a bumper sticker often seen in Europe these days,' Michael Pollan reports admiringly;[1] and it was his book, *The Omnivore's Dilemma*, that in 2006 kick-started a mainstream interest in the 'politics of the plate'.[2] Eating in the right foodist way is even now supposed, by the author of a book about *How Eight Cooks Saved My Life* (really?), to be 'the most political act we can commit'.[3]

Take the hottest food-ethics subject of recent years, the 'trend' or 'style'[4] for 'local' eating, aka 'locavorism': eating only what has been produced locally. Locavores don't all agree on what counts as 'local': some try to keep to eating food that was grown within a radius of 100 miles from the place of eating ('100-milers'), while for others it is enough that the food be 'nationally sourced', as with the London restaurant chain Canteen. René Redzepi, cook at 'world's best restaurant' Noma in Denmark, is a high-profile agitator for localism, though for him 'local' extends into a kind of pan-Scandinavian food nationalism: he 'uses only food from Sweden, Norway, Iceland, Denmark (including Greenland and the Faroe Isles) and Finland'.[5] (The science brigade, led by Heston Blumenthal, are by contrast decidedly anti-local, as Harold McGee explains admiringly in his foreword to *The Fat Duck Cookbook*: 'Cooks can now read on the Internet about a rare spice from the other side of the planet and a texture thickener from the snack-food industry, and have both on their stove-top in a few days.')[6]

Whatever 'local' eating actually means, a lot of its devotees insist that it is urgently necessary. Environmentalist David Suzuki is not a rhetorical outlier in saying: 'Eating locally isn't just a fad – it may be one of the most important ways we save ourselves and the planet.'[7] As is often the case, however, the mission to save the planet comes at the expense of a lot of less fortunate people struggling right now to live on it. The trouble is that locavores are refusing to buy food from the people who most need their custom: that is, poor farmers in the 'developing' world or global South. The philosopher Peter Singer and co-author Jim Mason do the math and argue: 'If you have a dollar to spend on beans and you can choose between buying locally grown beans at a farmers' market or beans grown by a poor farmer in Kenya – even if the local farmer would get to keep the entire dollar and the Kenyan farmer would get only two cents from your dollar – you will do more to relieve poverty by buying the Kenyan beans.'[8] From a global perspective, locavorism begins to look like a narcissistic pseudo-moralistic club for the wealthy to keep food and money circulating among their own tight little cliques.

The other problem with locavorism, as with neo-agrarian fantasies of 'organic' everywhere, is that it doesn't scale. Some locavores, like some 'organic' fanatics and 'deep ecologists', appear not to want everyone to be able to eat, as they think the world is overpopulated already. They are explicitly haters of civilization, misanthropic pastoralists. As Michael Pollan relates his exchange with farmer Joel Salatin: 'When I asked how a place like New York City fit into his vision of a local food economy he [replied]: "Why do we have to have a New York City? What good is it?"'[9] So it goes. The journalist and former locavore James E. McWilliams concludes after his investigations that you just can't 'universalize' the 'eat local' movement.[10] One simple reason is that many countries don't have enough water to grow enough crops to feed themselves: international trade in crops is an efficient way to redistribute the 'virtual water' they contain more evenly around the world.[11]

Locavorism is also thought to be a weapon against global

warming, since viands that don't have to travel as far to the foodist's gaping maw are responsible for fewer transport-related carbon-dioxide emissions. But the story is complicated: for a start, food transport both to Britain and within it is responsible for only 2.3 per cent of the country's emissions,[12] and locavorism can actually lead to an increased carbon footprint. British tomatoes grown in heated greenhouses and eaten outside of the normal season by a British person are responsible for three times the emissions caused by tomatoes trucked from Spain.[13] Taking into account emissions at all stages of production, it turns out to be 'four times more energy-efficient for London consumers to buy grass-fed lamb imported by ship from New Zealand than to buy grain-fed lamb raised locally'.[14]

Eating local, then, harms the world's poorest farmers, can't feed the world, and can exacerbate global warming. So why do it? The best reasons for locavorism, it turns out, are emotional, as Michael Pollan reveals: 'I'm thinking of the sense of security that comes from knowing that your community, or country, can feed itself; the beauty of an agricultural landscape; the outlook and kinds of local knowledge that farmers bring to a community; the satisfactions of buying food from a farmer you know rather than the supermarket.'[15] It's nice for him that Pollan was thinking of all those satisfying and pretty things, but none of them quite amounts to a slam-dunk ethical reason for what is supposed to be an ethical practice.

The best, perhaps, to be said for locavorism is that getting to know the farmer who grows one's food represents an admirable attempt to restore a sense of 'community' to the alienated urban landscape. It is a nice historical irony. Where the novels of Zola and Balzac are all about escaping the bigoted, narrow horizons of the local (including an exclusively local diet), now the local, it seems, is the utopian 'village' everyone dreams of returning to, the last place of social refuge. Here dies the great dream of cosmopolitanism. Similarly, locavorism can also count (again quite understandably) as a symbolic protest against the perceived evils of international commerce, a kind of fuck-the-system thrill. So two Vermont cheesemakers say that making cheese is 'their personal response to globalization'.[16] The use of food as political currency goes back at least to the moment in the late 1950s when the US changed the name of its 'Food Aid' programme to 'Food for Peace', but globalization probably won't notice the dissident action of two cheesemakers.[17] As Pat Benatar nearly sang: Stop using cheese as a weapon. (No doubt Alex James is, as I write, working on an AK-47-shaped cheese.)

Hardly any self-declared 'locavores' are able to keep to a rigorous 100-mile plan if that involves giving up sugar, coffee, wheat, and chocolate, as it did for Alisa Smith and J.B. MacKinnon, a pair of Canadians who, with truly impressive fortitude, followed a strictly 'local' diet for a year and wrote it up in the book *Plenty*. More common is a kind of fashion-statement pseudo-localism, as with a pair of dinner-party-throwing Manhattanites awarded a spread of adoring colour puffery by the *New York Times* style supplement: 'The couple are locavores in the neighborhood sense of the word. They get cheeses like goat cheddar and Solé gran queso from Murray's and pasta from Raffetto's; for meat, like pork tenderloin, they go to Faicco's.'[18] It must be admitted that it's a rather attenuated sense of 'locavores' that just means people who buy their food in fancy local shops.

Whether it's locavorism, 'organics', or some other species of world-changing foodism, the deeper problem with food ethics is one that it shares with all so-called ethical consumerism (or what Singer and Mason call 'conscientious consumption'): the idea that, in choosing what kind of commodity you buy, you are helping to improve society. It is really a decadent individualism: like a former public utility, the ethical question becomes privatized and mediated by market forces. The sociologists Josée Johnston and Shylon Baumann offer a pointed redescription: 'The market – in the form of educated and enlightened consumer choices – is presented as a solution for market failure.'[19]

The point is not that one shouldn't care whether one's dinner was tortured, or how many Chinese workers died to make one's iPad, but that simply shopping differently is not going to be the answer. For the self-congratulatory ethical consumer, though, too onerous an exercise of reason is avoided in favour of a comforting ethically packaged hedonism, as was admitted already in Frances Moore Lappé's eco-hippy-veggy manifesto of 1971, *Diet for a Small Planet*: 'The appeal to me has been more to my feelings than my rationality [. . .] eating habits can have a meaning, a meaning that not only feels closer to you than an abstract ethic but brings you pleasure too.'[20] People who really want to do something about the inequities of the world food economy tend to set up or support NGOs that campaign for changes in subsidies, tariffs, and other 'uneven' features of international trade, perhaps under the umbrella term 'food justice'.[21] They know that individuals choosing what to eat for dinner just can't make the right kind of difference overall. Ethical consumerism, on the other hand, gives up on the governmental approach to the collective-action problem and offers nothing in its place except a private warm glow of moral righteousness. As with 'sweatshop-free' clothing labels, ethical virtue is baked into the product, becoming itself a commodity.[22]

Foodist values are always in flux, as the hungry Francophile belletrist Adam Gopnik notes: 'A hundred years ago, for instance, one way to show you were a wise and knowing eater was to have out-of-season food. You had strawberries in December: showed you had access to them. Now that same kind of wise or knowing eater, or one who believes that he is, will have only seasonal food, only things that are entirely fresh and local, and so on. [. . .] These things cycle round again and again.'[23] That the nostrums of modern 'ethical' foodism are so noticeably inversions of the values of the past is no argument against them, but it does contextualize their status as fashionable concerns, however sincerely they might be held. Another turn of the cycle can be seen in the up-to-the-minute locavorist subtrend of 'foraging', or collecting and eating what happens to be lying around on the forest floor or beach. Once that was strictly for the poor who had no other option; but by 2011, an editorial in *Gastronomica* magazine could note: 'Already, within the past year or so, for food to be deemed truly authentic, it has to be foraged by hand.'[24] It was reported elsewhere that the multibillionaire Facebook founder Mark Zuckerberg was 'eating only what he kills this year'.[25] (The purveyor of this delectable factoid, tucked away in a technology story about a hot Silicon Valley startup, did not tell us whether Zuckerberg was personally murdering his own lettuce and potatoes as well as whatever animals he was consuming.)

Foraging is also trumpeted as a virtuous activity by none other than René Redzepi, of the pseudo-localist restaurant Noma, who is the hero of a *New Yorker* essay on the topic. The reporter Jane Kramer notes that foraging 'has become so fashionable a subject in the past few years that one eater.com blogger called this the era of the "I Foraged with René Redzepi Piece"'.[26] Nothing daunted, Kramer goes on to write her own 'I foraged with René Redzepi' piece. Before she gets to the meeting with Redzepi, she notes that once upon a time, 'foraged food was a sign of poverty';[27] her initial examples of what now counts as foraging make it seem, by contrast, rather like a hobby for the wealthy. Her American summer neighbours keep 'truffle hounds' who annoyingly scarf her own truffles while she is 'back in New York'. She goes foraging with some foodists who live in an 'Oxfordshire farmhouse' with a 'vast' garden; the husband (by delightful coincidence, one of the authors of *The Official Foodie Handbook*) is left 'in charge of fetching claret from the cellar and coaxing heat from an unpredictable Aga'.[28] What could be more agreeable? (In a pleasant twist of lexicographical history, to 'forage', back in 1593, meant 'to glut oneself, as a wild beast'.)[29]

The reader is finally introduced to Redzepi himself, described, incredibly, as 'arguably the most famous Dane since Hamlet'.[30] Only a monocultural food-maniac could think this: at least, I wager that Lars Von Trier, Helena Christensen, Whigfield, Peter Høeg, Niels Bohr, and Søren Kierkegaard are all considerably more famous. Redzepi learned his craft at Ferran Adrià's El Bulli and Thomas Keller's French Laundry, and then founded his 'Nordic Food Lab' to research the wild foods of his region. Through foraging, he tells Kramer, 'I got connected to the sea and soil, and now they're an integral part of me. I experience the world through food.'[31] (One wonders in passing if this means that a dedicated foodist's other senses are somehow attenuated by the monstrous growth of the gustatory organ: whereas most of us are lucky enough also to experience the world through vision, hearing, and touch, a foodist can experience the world only by putting it in his mouth, like a giant baby.) Personally rewarding as 'foraging' might be, it turns out that Redzepi's restaurant operation now depends for the supply of most of its 'local' ingredients on an army of 'professional foragers', which rather undercuts the heroically Emersonian image of the redoutable food-gatherer.[32]

The real 'foraging' in our age, of course, is done by those people who rummage in supermarket dustbins: it is the liberation and putting-to-use of all the perfectly edible food that the large chains throw away every day – when they do not, obscenely, deliberately spoil it by slashing open the packaging or soaking it in dye before putting it in the bins, in order to discourage its eating.[33] The search for this kind of food is, revealingly, not generally known as 'foraging' but as dumpster-diving or 'freeganism'. The kind of foodist foraging celebrated in the *New Yorker*, by contrast, is really just about a pleasant way to interact aesthetically with nature in the company of like-minded people, with the promise of a nice meal at the end of it. In other words, foraging is the foodist equivalent of golf.

11.

The Great Escape

Foraging is a day-trip escape into the friendly and abundant larder of nature, and food can also provide escapism in the sense of that term we apply to entertainment. It enables you to escape mentally from your dreary physical surroundings, or from the present moment: back into distant history, or into your own early youth. As Lin Yutang, popularizer of Chinese philosophy to America in the twentieth century, put it: 'What is patriotism but the love of good things we ate in our childhood?'[1] Many famous cooks now take 'inspiration' from what they ate as nippers, to swaddle the customers in a cosy reverie. Heston Blumenthal writes: 'Nostalgia often influences my development of recipes for the Fat Duck – the tasting menu features, among other things, versions of the sherbet dab and coconut baccy.'[2] Appealing to health-conscious foodists' fond memories of their student sustenance must be part of the thinking behind the new wheeze of 'gourmet' Pot Noodle-style instant noodle pots called 'Wholesome Pots' launched in the UK in 2011. Whereas your actual Pot Noodle came in no-nonsense flavours such as 'Chicken' (though I am staggered now to discover that it was only ever virtual-reality poultry, since 'All Pot Noodle flavours are 100% suitable for vegetarians'),[3] the 'Wholesome Pots' of grains and pulses launched by 'The Food Doctor' come in flavours such as 'bulgar wheat and quinoa with tomato, black olive and basil', 'asparagus, leek and mint', and 'couscous and lentils with tomato, red pepper and cumin'.[4] In this way one may happily indulge the nostalgia of making 'food' by pouring boiling water into a plastic pot of freeze-dried matter.

At the Chicago restaurant Next in late 2011, Grant Achatz and Dave Beran unveiled, to much foodist swooning, a ten-course 'Childhood Menu'. Present and correct are the high-foodist's ironic scare-quotes (the 'Chicken "Noodle" Soup' contains no actual noodles), the kitschy serving ideas (one course is sold in a 1980s 'vintage' plastic lunchbox featuring Knight Rider or Gremlins), and the neo-Futurist multisensory experience (a course called 'Campfire' is actually a fire at your table). The 'concept' is authoritarian: you *shall* have childhood memories while eating this stuff.[5] It is perhaps worthwhile to note that Marcel Proust's madeleine did not inspire in him a yielding to insipid retro-infantilism but drove him to spend years concentrating ferociously in a cork-lined room in order to compose an enormous novel. Next's Childhood menu would surely be the ideal gastronomic overture for the wealthy businessman who plans later to go back to his hotel with an 'escort' and dress up in a nappy.

Foodist nostalgia does not have to be for one's own childhood in particular. In her preface to the second edition of *A Book of Mediterranean Food*, Elizabeth David admits that when it was first published in 1950, 'almost every essential ingredient of good cooking was either rationed or unobtainable'. Her readers, therefore, could not cook from it. But, she writes, it was 'stimulating' even so to 'think about' the recipes, 'to escape from the deadly boredom of queueing [. . .] to read about real food cooked with wine and olive oil, eggs and butter and cream'.[6] The incantatory power of ingredient names evidently achieved gastroporn status avant la lettre. Evelyn Waugh, meanwhile, said that he seasoned *Brideshead Revisited* with rich scenes of gourmandizing in order to 'console himself for the kind of food he was actually eating while writing the novel during the war years'.[7]

Foodist escapism can also be a psychic journey in space as well as time. Written foodism is very often a kind of travel literature (even when it isn't explicitly so, as *Eat, Pray, Love* and Anthony Bourdain's *A Cook's Tour* are). The tasting menu of the restaurant Alinea is actually called a 'tour' (how especially convenient for the swollen gulch, who can thereby journey exotically without leaving his well-upholstered chair); Australia's leading glossy foodist periodical is named *Gourmet Traveller*. In 2008, *Saveur* magazine announced that 'gastro-tourism is one of the fastest growing segments of the travel industry'.[8] Increasingly many people voyage at the dictates of the stomach, and talk exclusively about what they consumed when they return. (Look out for my forthcoming horror movie about a nubile gang of holidaying foodists being murdered one by one: *I Still Don't Care What You Ate Last Summer*.)

Travelling to far-flung climes just to stuff one's face has always been an elite enterprise, ever since the Greek author of the *Deipnosophists*, Athanaeus, looked askance at one ancient foodist author's research strategy: 'But this Archestratus was so devoted to luxury, that he travelled over every country and every sea with great diligence, wishing, as it seems to me, to seek out very carefully whatever related to his stomach.'[9] Unfortunately Archestratus was a dull kind of foodist puritan, warning his readers: 'Have nothing to do with those Syracusans who simply drink, like frogs, without eating anything.' (The Syracusans sound like fun, don't they?) More congenial is Lieutenant-Colonel Newnham-David's 1903 *Gourmet's Guide to Europe* (co-written with one Algernon Bastard), where it is recommended that breakfast should consist of Vermouth, crabs, scampi risotto, truffles, cheese, and a bottle of Valpolicella, plus a glass of champagne for the chap and one of Alkermes for his consort. The authors reassure the reader: 'The Maître d'Hôtel will be interested in you directly he finds that you know how a man should breakfast.'[10] One day, I promised myself on reading this, I shall breakfast thus.

Even if one is not journeying imaginatively, food can

still give comfort, particularly in straitened economic times: it offers a kind of dependability when all else is in unpredictable flux. The journalist Richard Godwin noticed that many of his friends in their thirties could not afford to buy flats and had delayed having children; instead they posted pictures of their meals on Facebook. 'To be kind,' he concluded, 'you could say we use food to provide comfort that's lacking elsewhere.'[11] Over the previous decade, Britain had experienced two bubbles: one in property, the other in food. Perhaps a continuing dedication to the latter, not yet burst, was compensation for having missed out on the former.

Seeing no doubt this foodism-as-security as the next submarket waiting to be tapped, two of the star cooks most famous for their zanily elaborated, super-expensive 'molecular' restaurant food both published, in late 2011, books about home cooking. Perhaps eating in was going to be the new eating out, as it had previously become during the recessions of the 1930s and then the early 1990s, when 'home cooking – now called "comfort food" – became the name of the game', and an earlier new wave of basic cookbooks was published.[12] The 2011 versions add the glamour of a top avant-garde cook's expertise brought to bear on basic food that, so it is promised, you can actually cook in your own kitchen without needing plastic explosives and a small nuclear reactor. *Heston Blumenthal At Home* includes recipes for 'Scotch Eggs', 'Onion Soup', and 'Shepherd's Pie', but also some more elaborate stuff such as 'Konbu-cured Halibut' or

'Oxtail Faggots with Celeriac Purée'. Heston being Heston, he can't help advising the prospective home cook to invest at least in a 'digital probe', a 'cream whipper', and (*mais bien sûr*) a blowtorch.[13] Ferran Adrià's *The Family Meal*, illustrated with old-school step-by-step pictures, contains recipes for cheeseburgers and potato salad, and instructs the reader how to boil an egg, as had Delia Smith's *How to Cook* thirteen years previously. (I should here declare an interest, for it was from Delia's refreshingly straightforward manual that I first learned how to cook rice, and also a rather good Spanish omelette.) In a publicity interview, Adrià said: 'There has never been so much information and talking about cooking and yet few people cook at home any more. [. . .] It is not just a British problem. [. . .] [people] feel they can't afford to eat well when they are only earning 1,000 or 1,500 euros a month.'[14]

If Adrià is right, then the explosion of media foodism over the past few decades really has all been about porn, or snobbery, or escapism, or some combination of other factors, if the millions of people watching the cookery programmes and buying the cookery books have not been, well, cooking. Indeed, in Thomas Keller's second book, *Ad Hoc at Home*, he describes the food therein as 'approachable', and the recipes as 'doable at home',[15] thus implicitly admitting that few readers would have actually cooked anything from his first book, the superdeluxe foodist calling card that was *The French Laundry Cookbook*. *Ad Hoc At Home* is desperate to be more friendly, featuring big Photoshop montages of a grinning Thomas

Keller head in front of blackboards. On one such blackboard is scrawled the slogan 'I DO LOVE TO SPOON', while Keller, lovingly examining a spoon, speech-bubbles: 'I love spoons the way I love eggs, for the beauty of their shape and their multiple uses.'[16] (The British satirical magazine *Private Eye* has a long-running pretend-interview feature called 'Me and My Spoons', in which a celebrity is asked about their relationship with spoons. The final question is always 'Has anything amusing ever happened to you in connection with a spoon?', and the answer is nearly always 'No'. But they have never done Thomas Keller.)

So would Adrià and Co.'s new wave of comforting back-to-basics literary foodism encourage more people to begin cooking when previous waves of exactly the same thing didn't? One might be sceptical. Two decades previously, Marco Pierre White wrote in the impishly confrontational introduction to *White Heat*: 'You're buying *White Heat* because you want to cook well? Because you want to cook Michelin stars? Forget it. Save your money. Go and buy a saucepan.'[17] The latest collection of home-cooking manuals, too, can be seen mainly as a source of comfort porn, a dream of domestic self-sufficiency in a well-equipped home insulated from the terror and 'austerity' of the world outside.

12.

Time, Gentlemen, Please

Nothing good can be had quickly, or so goes the modern high-foodist philosophy. Cooking, and eating, should take time: lots of time. Such a view unites the apparently contradictory foodist groupings of slow-food organic locavores on the one hand and lab-coated cook-ringmasters on the other. In *The French Laundry Cookbook*, Thomas Keller writes: 'The recipes in this book are about wanting to take the time to do something that I think is priceless. Our hunger for the twenty-minute gourmet meal [. . .] has severed our lifeline to the satisfactions of cooking.'[1] Interminable foodist cooking is to whipping up something in the frying pan as Sting's tantric sex is to Jong's zipless fuck: in both cases, the (male) assumption is that the longer it takes, the better it will be.

Though it seems to be the British writer Christopher Driver who first coined the phrase 'slow food' in 1983, when describing his own preference for 'eating well, even if it means taking time and paying attention',[2] the formal Slow Food movement originated in Italy, and now runs its own University of Gastronomic Science. You will struggle to find an entire university anywhere devoted exclusively to mathematics, say, or literature, or chemistry; but of course food is more important than that. Michael Pollan approves: 'Slow Food offers a coherent protest against, and alternative to, the Western diet and way of eating, indeed to the whole ever-more-desperate Western way of life.'[3]

But who has the time? The problem is that the people most able to engage in such a 'protest' are the time-rich, which is to say mainly the rich, or those who have already best profited from the 'desperate Western way of life'. If you don't work long hours in a job (or maybe two) in order to make ends meet, then you probably can cook all your meat 'sous vide' for twenty-four hours. You can perhaps spend, as Heston Blumenthal once did on television, an hour and a half making mashed potatoes with 'eight different pots and utensils' to end up with something resembling 'thick soup'.[4] Slow-foodist strictures represent for the majority unable actually to follow them a fantasy of being both time-rich and cash-rich (in order to afford the recondite ingredients): this is the way one would eat, perhaps, as part of a modern rentier lifestyle.

Foodists write countless paeans to prolonged cooking sessions, or the virtue attendant upon a ventripotent blowout of heroically extended gastrimargy (or, as Michael Pollan calls it, a 36-hour dinner party);[5] but the cannier entrepreneurs –

such as Ferran Adrià with his back-to-basics *The Family Meal*
– recognize that most ordinary people are time-starved, even
if they are committed foodists. What, then, are they actually
going to eat? What Thomas Keller sneers at as the idea of
the 'twenty-minute gourmet meal' is the only way to ease this
tension: so, Rachael Ray's *30 Minute Meals* on the Food Network
in the US, Nigel Slater's *The 30-Minute Cook* and Jamie Oliver's
30 Minute Meals in Britain, and many other guides to rapid
cuisine. (Shortly after its 2010 launch, *Jamie's 30 Minute Meals*
became the fastest-selling non-fiction book ever published
in the UK, and it still sold more than any other book in
2011 except the novel *One Day*.) Modern foodism is split
into an odd dichotomy: great effort or minimal effort, with
little in between. One strand sees its admired chief artisans
emphasizing the hours and hours of preparation necessary to
cook anything worth eating; the other is all about convenience.

Woe betide anyone, however, who takes the idea of
convenience to heart and buys a 'ready meal' from the
supermarket, a disgusting vice which in the eyes of all public
opiners about food is on a par with smoking. Having the
time to cook 'real' food is a form of power, and – as usual in
human relations – the ones with the power (time is on our
side) interpret the lack of it in others as their own fault: to
be powerless is the result of a moral failing. The ready meal is
sometimes assumed to be a peculiarly Anglo-Saxon vice, as by
Joanna Blythman, the enraged author of *Bad Food Britain*, who is
apparently unaware that the French have an entire chain, Picard,

devoted to (very tasty) frozen dishes and ready meals, and they are ubiquitous, too, in Spain and Italy.[6] (Indeed, Roland Barthes was reporting already in 1961 on the availability in France of 'canned "gourmet dishes"', with their 'paradoxical association of gastronomy and industrialization'.)[7] Blythman does then allow that some ready meals (endorsed by celebrity cooks such as the pioneering gastroporn artiste Paul Bocuse) are available in mainstream French supermarkets, but fails to draw the obvious lesson: you can hardly attribute this phenomenon to French ignorance about food. The 'ready meal', evidently, is not a symptom of insufficient foodist education in one country or another; it is the sign not of a debased food culture, but (if anything) of a debased work culture. In Britain and the rest of Europe, many people do not have the combination of time and mental energy to cook when they get home every evening, even if they would like to; and to add insult to this existential injury, they are told that if they eat ready meals then they are repulsive and ignorant. (Others, of course, just can't be bothered to cook.) But the disjunction between foodist fantasy and actual food habits is in many ways not so much a food-education issue as an economic one; just as the ghastly slop being served to British schoolchildren before Jamie Oliver came along was not so much a foodist issue as a privatization issue: the school-dinner companies were spending 36p per child per day[8] (or a quarter as much as was spent on feeding an army dog, albeit for all its meals)[9] so as to maximize profit.

To a holier-than-thou foodist, on the other hand, if you eat a ready meal, you can hardly be said to be eating at all. Michael Pollan defines 'food' exclusively as stuff your grandmother would have recognized as food,[10] implicitly consigning everything else – say, a Wagon Wheel, a microwavable chicken tikka masala, or a ready-made portion of 'Boursin stuffed kangaroo nachos with roasted avocado corn salad and huckleberry habanero demi-glace'[11] – to some evil category of Unfood. (So too with a new 'Bistro Box' sold by Starbucks, whose label says it is 'real food', unlike that fake stuff everywhere else.) But the only true Unfood is that which is literally indigestible, e.g. a spanner.

To avoid the embarrassing taint of 'convenience' (or 'processed', let alone 'junk') food, the ideal quick cuisine for the serious modern foodist must still involve some echo of menial labour, so that he may feel a spiritual connection to the labouring peasants of an imaginary golden age of ubiquitous food authenticity. If one is not to go 'foraging' with well-booted chums, one may avail oneself instead of the increasing popularity of what we could call 'inconvenience food'. In the run-up to Christmas 2011, for example, Waitrose was selling 'Delia's Classic Christmas Cake', a cake invented by Delia Smith that came in kit form, all the ingredients pre-weighed and separately packaged and 'ready to mix'. It is a brilliant concept. This Ikea-style self-assembly exploded cake-in-waiting was, naturally, more expensive than other boxed cakes which were already, well, cakes. One now pays a premium for the opportunity to participate in a portion of the labour required to make the product, whereas previously (as with flat-pack furniture) that was reason for a discount on ready-made prices.

As Delia's Classic Christmas Cake shows, the chance to play at working is itself now worth extra money, perhaps especially for those who feel alienated from the increasingly virtualized products of their increasingly virtualized labour during the normal workday. So the recession turn to home baking (*The Great British Bake-off*) might have been just one instance of a more generalized nostalgic attempt to recapture the pleasures of craft (*Kirstie's Handmade Britain*), a direct physical connection to the outcome of one's work. As Max Horkheimer put it in conversation with Theodor Adorno half a century ago: 'In actual fact [people's] free time does them no good because the way they have to do their work does not involve engaging with objects. This means that they are not enriched by their encounter with objects. Because of the lack of true work, the subject shrivels up and in his spare time he is nothing.'[12] The modern worker attempts re-enrichment in his spare time by engaging with food objects.

The superior foodist's disdain for convenience and fetish for labour-for-its-own-sake constitute an intriguing reversal of the previous historical trend for 'labour-saving' in the home. Many people over the years have expressed good reasons for remaining dissident in the face of the swelling tide of foodism. Cooking could once be thought of uncontroversially as the 'first and paramount duty' of women, as 'G.V.', the dyspeptic, misogynist and anti-Semitic author of the mid-nineteenth-century philippic *Dinners and Dinner-Parties*, had it. He was outraged that, instead, women were being encouraged to read books, 'learn[ing] things which it had been well for them they had never known'.[13] His view was still being echoed half a century later by a woman who wrote about food for the *Pall Mall Gazette*. Elizabeth Robins Pennell, author of the deep-purple foodist catechism *The Feasts of Autolycus: The Diary of a Greedy Woman* (1896), recommended that a young woman should forget about frivolities such as the 'picture show' or 'a new book', and devote all her thought to food. 'Why clamour for the suffrage, why labour for the redemption of brutal man, why wear, with noisy advertisment, ribbons white or blue, when three times a day there is a work of art, easily within her reach, to be created?'[14]

By the mid-twentieth century, however, the advent of a new 'processed' convenience food could be thought of as politically liberating: Christopher Driver notes that the appearance of breakfast cereals from the mid-1950s, for instance, 'saved women in employment the time their mothers had had to spend over the porridge saucepan and the frying pan'.[15] And it was a palatably subliminal feminism that enlivened Delia Smith's very first book, 1971's *How to Cheat at Cooking*. She was reacting to the media foodism that even then seemed excessive: 'If something tastes good, it is good.

If it only took 20 minutes to make, so what? The flood of cookery manuals, part-works and tele virtuosi seems to have convinced us all that we need to be frightfully painstaking.'[16] Instead her recipes advise the reader to sex up packet soups with cream, canned beans and cheese; to 'disguise' instant mash with butter and chives; or, for a chicken dish, to 'Make up the onion sauce according to the instructions on the packet.'[17] Introducing the section on rice, she confides reassuringly: 'Rice is a good way of avoiding vegetables altogether', which today would be tantamount to including heroin in a recipe.[18] But there's nothing wrong with cheating, à la Delia, if you know the game is already rigged. (In 2008, Delia published another book also called *How to Cheat at Cooking*, which – to much foodist scorn and wailing – advised the use of ready-grated Parmesan and tinned breadcrumbs or minced lamb.)[19]

One especial reason for not spending so much time in the kitchen might be that you want to be 'free to drink', as Caroline Blackwood and Anna Haycraft put it with splendid directness in the 1980 bohemian's cookbook, *Darling, You Shouldn't Have Gone to So Much Trouble*, which collects quick, cheating, or satirical recipes by such luminaries as Lucian Freud, Francis Bacon, Quentin Crisp, Sonia Orwell, Barbara Cartland, and Marianne Faithfull. Modern women are 'in a state of mutiny' against the excessive demands of kitchen work, the authors write. So go ahead and use 'Crosse & Blackwell's Vichyssoise and Campbell's consommé' as bases for other soups, and deploy a disguised instant mash.[20] And never apologize: 'Modesty is unbecoming in a cook and only stimulates the critical faculties of guests, the very faculties which should ideally be deadened by the plying of cocktails and good wine.'[21] More recently, the cook Antony Worrall Thompson has put things in uncommon perspective. In Britain, he has said, 'I think we've got a hard core of three million or so who really enjoy food and cooking. There are a lot of women who think "Thank God for chilled foods. I don't have to cook any more."'[22] By way of contrast to the British foodist's stereotype of continental Europeans happily cooking themselves delicious meals every day, moreover, it is perhaps worth noting that Xavier Marcel Boulestin, the French celebrity chef and cookbook author of the 1920s (previously interior designer to London's smart set, he practised his cooking in the war), reveals in his memoir that for years he never cooked himself a thing, preferring to eat in London restaurants every day.[23]

As women got bored with cooking in the second half of the twentieth century, men got into it. The superlative spy novelist Len Deighton tempted British males into the kitchen with his 1965 *Action Cook Book*, whose cover featured a revolver with a sprig of parsley poking from its barrel. It included Deighton's 'cookstrips' for the *Observer*, which arranged culinary instructions as dynamic comic strips featuring big actiony verbs ('1. ROAST a duckling [. . .] 7. POUR sauce . . .').[24] 'At the time, it was considered quirky and unnatural for a man to cook for himself at home,' John Walsh comments, 'but it soon acquired cachet: a female chore was suddenly recast as a male socio-sexual accomplishment.'[25] In the film of Deighton's novel *The Ipcress File*, Harry Palmer (Michael Caine) says to Sue Lloyd, by way of foreplay, 'I am going to cook you the best meal you have ever tasted in your life.' On the other side of the Atlantic, meanwhile, wine-glugging cook and practitioner of 'hedonism in a hurry', Graham Kerr, became celebrated as *The Galloping Gourmet* (1969–71), while later on in Britain, the amusingly rakish Keith Floyd came as a godsend to media producers who considered that he had 'rescued' TV cooking from a 'female ghetto'.[26]

The titillating equation of food with fighting in the *Action Cook Book*'s gun motif was no accident. Indeed, foodism can be made to appeal particularly to men of a wannabe-macho bent by saying that cooking is like war. Marco Pierre White boasts that his outfit at Harvey's is 'the hardest kitchen in Britain; it's the SAS of kitchens'.[27] Heston Blumenthal compares the cleaning of a squid to the cleaning of an assault rifle.[28] Anthony Bourdain refers to 'civilian society' (people who aren't cooks); while, in his kitchen, 'This is still the army. Ultimately, I want a salute and a "Yes, sir!".'[29]

Even the ultrasensitive novelist Jonathan Safran Foer, in his terrible, self-admiring, and abysmally reasoned book *Eating Animals* (the philosopher Peter Singer is still your go-to guy for the strong ethical case in favour of vegetarianism), agrees with George W. Bush that we are at war with the fish.[30] But wait a minute – if cooking in general is war, then the larger enemy must be food itself. Indeed, that premise is made explicit in the title of the jolly US television series *Man v. Food*, in which the presenter journeys around America taking up eating 'challenges' of obscene quantity or, say, absurd spiciness. At the end of each episode, the winner is declared: either 'Man' or 'Food'. This show represents in its very excess the perfection of modern media foodism. Regardless of the lip service paid to 'respecting' it, food is really the foe, and it must be defeated in a display of triumphant absorption-annihilation, in the manner of the Borg in *Star Trek*.

There might also, in the military-cooking topos, be phantastical pleasure for the reader in the reverie of perfect subjugation to another's will: in this way, the burden of choice and thought may be avoided. Jeffrey Steingarten, waggish author of *The Man Who Ate Everything*, confesses: 'I have a policy of slavishly adhering to another writer's instructions, at least the first time. And I love following orders.'[31] There is certainly something of the Hegelian master–slave dialectic in foodist culture. Hervé This announces: 'I dream one day of having the final say in the matter of bouillon.'[32] Well, sure, who doesn't? And Anthony Bourdain proposes: 'If cooking professionally is about control, eating successfully should be about submission.'[33] (What would it mean to eat *unsuccessfully*? Simply failing to get the food into one's mouth? Or being unable to scoff an entire TurBaconEpicCentipede?)

Going one better authority-wise than the idea of the cook as military commander is the idea of cook as God, literally able to conjure food into existence from the void. Perhaps the literary acme of the time-rich foodist's congratulation on her own supernatural artisanship is provided by the indefatigable Elizabeth Gilbert in *Eat, Pray, Love*:

> I [. . .] soft-boiled a pair of fresh brown eggs for my lunch. I peeled the eggs and arranged them on a plate beside the seven stalks of the asparagus [. . .] I put some olives on the plate, too, and the four knobs of goat cheese I'd picked up yesterday from the *formaggeria* down the street, and two slices of pink, oily salmon. For dessert – a lovely peach, which the woman at the market had given to me for free and which was still warm from the Roman sunlight. For the longest time I couldn't even touch this food because it was such a masterpiece of lunch, a true expression of the art of making something out of nothing.[34]

We who have never made a masterpiece of lunch out of nothing (except for the various food products that we have recently bought and put on a plate) can only kneel in drooling awe before this portrait of a solipsist goddess miracling her own sustenance from thin air, thus demonstrating perfect dominion not merely over other people but over the laws of nature themselves. But it would be unrealistic for the rest of us to aspire to recreate such feats, we who must live as mortals, dependent on one another. Indeed, what if cooking and eating, for ordinary humans, were characterized not as a duty of protracted labour, or as a war, or as a marathon contest of domination and submission, or as a sunlit sacrament of self-worship, but as a kind of collaboration – or even a party?

13.

Il Faut Bien Manger

Imagine you have just won the TV advertising account for Kentucky Fried Chicken, with a brief to nudge the brand upmarket. It's something of a challenge: you can't in good faith try pretending that the coated poultry and fries are inherently of comparable quality to those of some organic locavore heirloom chicken'n'chips house asking four times the price. So what do you do? In a stroke of inspiration, you come up with a slow-motion montage in home-movie saturated colour of a group of beautiful young people messing about in a garden, occasionally munching something not-too-recognizable from a KFC bucket, while wistful indie music plays. At the end comes your slogan of laconic literary genius:

the people
the moment
the taste
KFC

In other words, what's good about scoffing KFC is that you're having a good time with friends. And this commercial is not only effective but actually true. I would far rather eat KFC with one friend or many than eat the world's most expensive restaurant meal with people I didn't find simpatico. Lest I be accused of erecting false dichotomies, let me immediately allow that that is not the only choice we have: fine food with one or more loved ones is very pleasant too. But what foodist culture, in all the eldritch manifestations I have surveyed in this book, is always at risk of losing sight of is this: that what is really important is not the food, but the company. Delia Smith's original *How to Cheat at Cooking* is itself a charming manifesto for conviviality, which could with social profit be reissued today. 'What we may have lacked in the kitchen,' she points out with aplomb, 'we can make up for in the dining-room.'[1]

To be fair, this is a truth recognized by many modern foodists, although they sometimes take an odd route to get there. The American physician and writer Leon Kass wrote a book explicitly arguing for the spiritual value of food as a vehicle of conviviality, appropriately entitled *The Hungry Soul*. (In it, by way of introduction, he fulminates against the noxious modern trends of 'analytical clarity', 'logical consistency', and 'feminism', and claims that the theory of evolution is 'not incompatible' with the Book of Genesis. He later became the head of George W. Bush's Council on Bioethics.)[2] Kass notices (after Brillat-Savarin) that animals just feed; but humans sit down at tables and *dine*, and this shows, or so he thinks, that we are not 'merely' animals ourselves but exist on a higher spiritual plane. Yet we may tremble at the prospect of dining chez Kass: among the topics of conversation he sternly declares inappropriate for the dinner table are 'exchange of opinion', 'gossip', 'reports of the day's events', 'the mutual exchange of ideas', and 'ribaldry', which I think just about covers the kinds of chat at all the most enjoyable dinners I've ever had. Instead, eating with Kass seems a more Apollonian than Dionysian prospect: one is obliged to talk, in a 'light and convivial' way, about 'topics of general and common interest': this 'enables us to taste, indeed to savor, the souls of our fellow diners'.[3] The ingestion of food thus becomes merely the pretext for a much more alarming meal: spiritual cannibalism. Though Kass's arguments are too religiose for my taste, I do not wish to disagree with his emphasis on the conviviality of the dining table. But even according to his fruity celebrations of the higher pleasures of eating with one's fellow humans, it is not the eating itself that nourishes the soul, but the social intercourse.

'*Il faut bien manger*,' Jacques Derrida says, which means both 'we have to eat, after all' and 'we should eat well'. So how does one eat well? One eats, he says, with other people.[4] Just as wine and beer, according to Roger Scruton, embody 'social virtues' when drunk deliberatively with friends ('the practice of buying rounds in the pub,' he points out, 'is one of the great cultural achievements of the English'), so too with food.[5] A 'companion', according to the Latin etymology, is someone you share bread with; and a 'symposium' was an eating-and-drinking party with good conversation. (The Greeks were clear that, at dinner, the mind as well as the stomach must be present.)[6] Socrates would surely have approved mightily of the conceptual invention nearly two and a half millennia after his death by the French writer and musician Boris Vian of the 'pianocktail', a machine to mix drinks that would fit the music you are playing.[7] Not many kitchen gadgets could be more conducive to conviviality than that.

It must be noted here that a relative indifference to the food in favour of the conversation will not by itself guarantee an excellent dinner, at least if one plans one's soirées on the model once recommended by the pseudo-philosopher Alain de Botton. He prefers, so he wrote, to feed his guests ready meals ('grilled salmon with mashed potatoes bought ready made from M&S or Tesco'), the better to be able to quiz them: 'Good conversation,' he philosophizes, 'is when people make themselves vulnerable and reveal things about themselves that could be taken against them in the future.' This begins to seem a little more disturbing than the blandly general dinner conversation chez Leon Kass. 'I like the idea of singing for your supper,' de Botton continues menacingly. 'Sometimes in life you have to be prepared to give something of yourself.' In return for a ready meal, this might seem like rather a poor bargain; but be reassured that de Botton will also offer a little something to take the edge off. 'I don't drink much so I'm a bad host in that sense, but my dear wife Charlotte would take care of that with a bottle of red and a bottle of white.'[8] That's two bottles, between eight guests. Between the weird demand for personal exposure and the uncivil restriction of drink, one fears that conviviality is going to be rather challenged around de Botton's table so constituted. Or, as one *Guardian* commenter put it rather more vividly: 'His "perfect dinner party" strikes me as as the sort of thing a movie psychopath would hold to make his guests feel uncomfortable, just before murdering them.'[9]

Foodists do aspire to conviviality in some other ways. Perhaps the most admirable motivation of the locavore, as we have seen, is to make convivial once more the fractured city, to rebuild some kind of 'community' – if only around the buying and selling of food. (Though this arguably comes at the cost of global solidarity.) I'm sure it is fun, too, to go 'foraging' with a couple of mates; and foodists who consider food capable of rising to the level of art, or even of sex, no doubt find pleasure and reassurance in one another's company, as do members of all kinds of oddball subcultures.

The restaurant itself, only two and a half centuries old, enacts worries about the problem of conviviality by rhetorically promising an ersatz version of it. Restaurants and famous cooks almost always refer to their diners as 'guests'. Very well, then, if I am your guest, please allow me to express my gratitude for this superb nosh. I certainly owe you dinner. Oh, what's that? You have presented me with a bill? You want me to pay money for what I have eaten? That is not normally how one treats one's 'guests'. What I am to the restaurant, in truth, is not a 'guest' but a customer. The ubiquity of the implication that any true hospitality is involved (as, too, in hotels) does not neutralize the squeamish pretension of its desire to airbrush out the commercial nature of the enterprise; or, on a kinder interpretation, to psycholinguistically prime the ambience as one of conviviality. This has occurred, at least, to Noma restaurateur René Redzepi, who nobly says that he wishes his joint could be free, since 'there is nothing worse than charging people for conviviality'.[10] (Of course there are lots of worse things, like murder.) Meanwhile, one London restaurant, I am assured, promises that all its berries are 'hand-picked by Justin' in an allegedly nearby forest. Who is Justin? Nobody knows, but it's a disarmingly nice way to make the fruit, and the place, seem more friendly.[11]

Surveying the semiotics of French food culture in 1961, Roland Barthes espies 'a trace of the mythical conciliatory power of conviviality' in a surprising place: the 'business lunch', because its purpose, after all, is that of 'comfort and long discussions'. At the business lunch, he says, the 'gastronomic' or 'traditional' quality of the dishes is emphasized, but as a means to a distinct end: 'to stimulate the euphoria needed to facilitate the transaction of business'.[12] I don't attend enough of them to know myself, but I can't help wondering whether today the business lunch might still be a potentially more convivial occasion than the anxiously monothematic foodist's dinner party.

Or maybe cookbooks are helping, given that they are nearly all selling conviviality rather than mere roasting instructions. *Jamie's Great Britain* makes the unashamed promise: 'If you cook these recipes, you will be rewarded with good times, brilliant weekends and big smiles all around the table.'[13] The comfort for sale is not merely that of private gorging, but spreads throughout your social circle. Popularity and happiness have never been so cheap and easy to acquire: just the cost of a cookbook will do it. (Of course, true conviviality is not meted out like a teacher's sticky stars for good homework. If your dinner guests are friendly just to the extent that they consider the recipe to have been well executed, then you have probably invited the wrong people in the first place.) In Fergus Henderson's *Nose to Tail Eating*, meanwhile, the photographs are rather lovely: exclusively aerial views of a rough-hewn dining table, with several pairs of hands around it, gesticulating or reaching to grab unidentifiable bits of animal. It's an artfully choreographed evocation of good company.

In their book *Foodies*, the sociologists Josée Johnston and Shyon Baumann interview numerous self-described 'foodies' who insist not only that food is 'meaningful', but even that they 'live to eat rather than eat to live'.[14] Live to eat? Really? There is actually now a Twitter hashtag #livetoeat, under which rubric cyber-foodists can broadcast their latest gullet-stuffing to their salivating followers. Surely they mean it as a joke. Really living to eat would be a kind of despair, a denial of our rationality and creativity, a willing self-demotion to a status worse than bestial. (Even other animals do not live merely to eat; they play and socialize, as well as rearing their young.) To live to eat represents the apotheosis and dead end of individualist consumerism. The live-to-eaters, if they are really serious, are forever looking in the wrong place for their life's meaning: down at their plates rather than across to their companions. (Or even at a book, by means of which one may be convivial with the absent or deceased.) Isn't it all a bit sad? For the wisest corrective to the frantic foodism of our age, we need after all look no further than the century-old dictum of W.S. Gilbert: 'It isn't so much what's on the table that matters as what's on the chairs.'

14.

Envoi: Virtual Eating

A man walks past me talking excitedly on his mobile phone. 'Hi mate, we're in, we just blagged it!' This is not a rock concert or a music festival; it is MasterChef Live, a gigantic foodist exhibition, the epitome of a consumer show. Beneath the glass-and-iron vault of the Grand Hall of Olympia in London is a cornucopia of stands selling food, drink, and kitchen gadgetry. Butchers and farmers promote their wares at stands dressed up to look rustic, with strings of garlic hanging at the back. In tiny cough-medicine plastic cups one can taste Chocolate Wine (red wine adulterated with chocolate by a maniac), various spirits, and real ales. There are sausages and curries, chocolate and cupcakes, fudge and 'gourmet popcorn', a whole hog roast, and lots and lots of tea. Miniature toasts or squares of bread support the dégustation of pâté or flavoured rapeseed oil. Thousands of tiny groans of pleasure coalesce into a loud hum throughout the hall.

Lots of this food caters to 'health' or fashionable

'intolerances'. One of the most popular tea stands is for a 'weight-loss tea', which (probably not coincidentally) is staffed by the show's most glamorous assistants (or what the adolescent-male world of videogame expos calls 'booth babes'). The rapeseed-oil guy claims, perhaps optimistically, that his stuff is 'healthier than olive oil'; there is a stand for chocolate that contains no dairy products; and even a 'Free From' bakery, which specializes in cakes that contain no gluten, wheat, or dairy, and may even, if you wish, be liberated from sugar and eggs to boot. (What is left after all those things are taken out that could deserve the name of 'cake' is beyond my comprehension.) In the latest wheeze of 'convenience' food, I find that I can buy cartons of 'liquid egg white', so I will never again have to worry about what to do with those poisonous yolks. There is also a stand selling 'Conscious Food', which I worry at first might consist of live animals that I am invited to bite into while they are still wriggling and thinking. Luckily it turns out to be something 'ayurvedic', that cures indigestion and probably unhappiness.

There are also a lot of educational establishments offering courses. A 'School of Artisan Food' is up-to-the-moment in its projected curriculum, which includes 'Baking', 'Chocolate', and 'Preserves & Pickling'. No doubt the author of the nineteenth-century foodist polemic *Dinners and Dinner Parties* is looking down with approval on this promised return to his golden age, before females were subjected to useless education on subjects other than cooking.

The foodist gadgets range from the expensive to the ridiculous. The best slogan is definitely 'Kin Knives – Kin Sharp'; elsewhere one can watch expert demonstrators enthral small crowds with their market patter while working a Gourmet Cheese Mill, or a Miracle Shammy (*sic*, for 'chamois'). There is a hypnotic stand showing 'pop-up storage solutions': motorized spice racks that rise from your work surface and whirr down again when done. A couple of beefy men smile ironically while the racks move up and down under their hands to the accompaniment of inspirational pounding music. There are Toastabags (make a toasted sandwich in a bag, in a normal toaster), and a big stand of massage chairs, including those that massage your feet and ankles, perfect for the sluggish metabolism of the overindulged foodist grazer. Over at one sad side, a man is demonstrating a steam iron, by ironing clothes. When I try to photograph a man hawking a thing called the Nicer Dicer (it dices things, apparently nicer), he starts shouting at me assertively to the effect that no photographs are allowed. 'Sir, I'd rather you didn't, please,' Nicer Dicer man bellows, not very nicely. I snap the photograph anyway and walk off briskly with my precious industrial secret, dreaming of selling it to the Chinese.

At the far end of the hall is the 'Restaurant Experience' which, like any capital-E Experience, is not the real thing but a sanitized and edited simulacrum of it. Stalls are offering 'pop-up' versions of famous restaurants: Roast, Gauthier Soho, Theo Randall at the Intercontinental. You buy a microscopic version of one of their 'signature' dishes on a ten centimetre-diameter polystyrene plate, for five or six quid, and then eat it at a trestle table. Cunningly, however, no cash changes hands directly with the servers. First you have to convert your money into Dining Currency, which comes in the form of translucent red poker chips. Then you give your chips in return for food (sadly, no one has chips), and if you have any chips left, you cash them in afterwards. Thus the Dining Experience attempts to recreate the subtle cognitive shunt of the casino: with chips in your hand, you feel less as though you are playing with real, hard-earned cash, and so are more likely to give it all back to the house. Wary of what I immediately espy as this psychological manipulation, I buy exactly six units of Dining Currency, all of which I exchange for a tiny bowl of braised octopus and chorizo with chickpeas in a spicy tomato sauce, from Smith's of Smithfield. It is surprisingly bland, but that might well be because I am eating it out of a foam bowl in the middle of a deafening exhibition hall rather than off fine tableware in a pleasantly dim room. In any case, I now regret not buying two hog-roast sandwiches upstairs in the 'Producer's Village' for the same price.

Oh, did I mention the cars? In the hall is a large Jaguar stand with several Jaguar cars on display. I don't think they are left over from a previous *Top Gear* exhibition, but what they have to do with foodism I am not able quite to fathom, apart from the printed slogans saying 'Jaguar à la carte' (concept: you can choose from different models of Jaguar, as from different dishes on a menu), and perhaps that the show in general has been expecting a particularly wealthy kind of visitor. Certainly most of the crowd look well-heeled if not always well upholstered. There are fashionable young couples, parents wheeling round babies in expensive military-chic buggies (foodist babies being, as we know, the hot accessory of the moment), and young people with their mothers, or whole families of stylish mum and dad with excited teenage children. What distinguishes this from a rock concert is that you're not embarrassed to go with your parents.

As with a rock concert, however, there is a lot of live performance. In the centre of the hall is the massive MasterChef Live Challenge, in which lucky customers are stood behind several cooking set-ups in an imitation of the TV show, while the presenter goes around and slurps their efforts. There are also smaller cooking stages: the Luce Cooking Stage and the MasterChef Demonstration Stage Sponsored by Sainsbury's. Since the only noise allowed here is the verbal naming of tastes and the smacking of lips, you cannot hear the guitarist playing at the Carte Noire 'lounge' unless you sit down and don the headphones supplied for the purpose. There are no free places, so I just watch him without headphones as though it's a mime performance. (It's very good.) This panoply of live cooking on the show floor is all very well, but to experience the full effect of in-your-face, in-the-moment performance foodism I have booked a ticket to the exclusive Chef's Theatre, whither I now make my way.

We 200-odd ticket-holders for this timetabled show of 'Live Cook Theatre' file in to a beautiful old marble-columned room, which I fantasize once hosted educational lectures or chamber-music concerts, and take our seats on hard folding plastic chairs. The violet-lit stage hosts two cooking set-ups and is labelled at the sides 'With Thanks to Belling, Lec, Magimix', causing me to suspect that the whole affair is a brilliantly synergistic exercise in product placement, which thought is not dismissed by the fact that on a giant screen above the stage are now projected several minutes of adverts, beginning with a hard-sell invitation to buy your tickets now for next year's MasterChef Live show, and continuing with promotions for the MasterChef Academy App (for iPhone and iPad), the Jaguar XJ (a kind of motor car), and Sainsbury's, thanks to whose generosity one may 'Live Well for Less'.

At length an MC, with an enthusiastic live-TV announcer's voice, announces: 'Please welcome to the Chef's Theatre Sponsored by Sainsbury's . . . your host, Andy Friedlander!' The lights and the audience go crazy. Friedlander informs us that we will be seeing live cooking done by the news broadcaster and *Celebrity MasterChef* success Kirsty Wark, as well as the Michelin-starred Scottish cook Tom Kitchin. First we watch a heartwarming video montage of Wark's plate-tastic moments on last year's television show, and then she arrives stage left, to blasts of (for some reason) deafening funk music. Kitchin arrives afterwards, and it is explained to us that they will both be cooking something with raw salmon, which they then start doing, chopping and heating ingredients while Friedlander engages them in foodist chat. Kitchin is very engaging: a bit like a nice version of Mick Hucknall, with a pleasant line in appearing to deflate foodist pretensions while still reserving the right to adopt them. (He'll add shallots and 'micro-herbs' to 'make it cheffy'.) Wark confides to us that you should use hot milk for mashed potato. I end up watching most of the performance on the giant screen, which is the only way you can see what the cooks are actually doing, as well as because I am near the back and there is no rake to the seating: thus is recreated the authentic experience of watching cooking on television, except with markedly more uncomfortable chairs.

At one point a smiling Wark offers what is probably the best possible defence of our cookery-mad media. 'Cooking is such a joy,' she explains. 'It's something you can learn and become better at.' This is certainly true; but the aggregate weight of foodist media in our culture surely goes beyond all possible educational value. If you just want to get better at cooking, you can do that in a few weeks or months by buying a few cookbooks and practising. You can also learn and get better at playing the cello or tailoring, but we are not so inundated by mass pseudo-education on those topics (though we do have the excellent US show *Project Runway* for the aspiring fashionista). Instead, a lot of food shows are really a subspecies of reality TV, the appeal of which is getting to know the contestants and (in its competitive form) rooting for your favourite. *Come Dine with Me*, in particular, has gradually slackened its focus on the actual food swallowed by the characters: instead, it is in the business of promulgating a rather socially inspirational narrative arc, repeatedly demonstrating that people who rub you up the wrong way are probably perfectly nice once you get to know them a little better.

Back in the Live Cook Theatre, Tom Kitchin has been lining a metal ring with thinly sliced cucumber and then chucking his minced salmon tartare into the middle. When he gently lifts the ring off, leaving the cucumber-wall standing firm, the audience lets out an amazed 'Aaaah!' and a round of applause, as though he had produced a live rabbit from a pan of boiling water, or sawn Kirsty Wark in half. An intact Wark tastes Kitchin's dish and pronounces it delicious, gamely attempting the obligatory gustatory phenomenology: 'I've got the shallot . . . then the salmon comes through.' But this is the strangely hermetic climax on all TV cookery shows: the moment when the judge or cook tastes the finished food on our behalf, yet cannot make us share the taste sensations. It is where gastroporn reveals itself to be tragically less stimulating than porn: though the consumer of sex porn cannot know intimately the exact feelings of the actors, she can induce in herself contemporaneously what she supposes to be an analogous experience. But I cannot taste Tom Kitchin's salmon tartare, especially when I am sitting in the same room as it, since there was no chance I could have cooked along with him – but then, almost no one does that while watching it on TV either. So the tasting finale of all cookery shows is a curious kind of pleasure by proxy: our on-screen representative has all the incommunicable fun on our behalf. Watching *Project Runway*, we can have an opinion about the clothes on show at the end of each episode, since both we and the judges are just looking at them. But for a cooking show we have to outsource our sensory apparatus and with it our faculty of judgement. It is virtual eating.

Jean Baudrillard would not have been surprised that virtual eating should prove more expensive than actual eating. I'm in the 'Bronze' seats at the back and have paid £15; the 'Gold' punters at the front have paid £25 for this show, or nearly a pound a minute: after a fraction over half an hour, the Live Cook Theatre is over, to star-struck applause, and we file out again to the accompaniment of a repeat of the Sainsbury's advert, set with savage irony to the song 'Bare Necessities'. The invention of *MasterChef* itself in 1990 was all about the 'democratisation of food', or so its creator Franc Roddam (also the director of the film *Quadrophenia*) has said. 'At that point good food was only for rich people. It was like, "No, hang on a second. Let's democratise this."'[1] But his baby seems by now to have grown into an oligarchic monster, and I'm in its belly.

It turns out that something like the Live Cook Theatre was once imagined, and described in the subjunctive of comic implausibility, by C.S. Lewis:

You can get a large audience together for a strip-tease act — that is, to watch a girl undress on the stage. Now suppose you come to a country where you could fill a theatre by simply bringing a covered plate on to the stage and then slowly lifting the cover so as to let every one see, just before the lights went out, that it contained a mutton chop or a bit of bacon, would you not think that in that country something had gone wrong with the appetite for food?[2]

We all live in that country now, our most desired stars of stage and screen all those colourfully 'styled' and virtually tasty morsels of supererogatory sustenance.

It is the golden hour, as the setting late-autumn sun shines warmly through the glass roof of Olympia, built at the British Empire's peak and now full of post-Empire Britons indulging while they still can in a kind of imperialism of the taste buds. I consider that I have earned a tour around 'The Wine Show', an area of MasterChef Live devoted to the Bacchic pleasures. I get a wine glass (made of actual glass) and walk around, taking a snifter of Burgundy here, or a 'Bordeaux-style' Languedoc there. The tasting bars here are crowded, and people are growing noticeably more aggressive in their elbowing to the front. Most of the punters, it seems, are by now getting a little tired and emotional after a whole Sunday of foodist munching, becoming pissed on multiple last sips from the bottom of a self-emptying receptacle and barging their way to the next tilted bottle, whatever the hell is in it. There are some long-booked-up educational tasting sessions and a workshop on how to pair wine with food (my philosophy: eat food; drink what you like with it, as long as it's French), and also, for reasons I do not comprehend, a stand for Qatar Airways.

I reflect almost soberly on what I have learned from my immersion in the warm bain-marie of foodist culture. Well, the top cooks seem to agree that Bird's Eye frozen peas are the best peas to use (the frozen ones are frozen so quickly after picking that, once thawed, they will be fresher than 'fresh' peas). And it's a waste of olive oil to cook with it, at least according to Thomas Keller.[3] More generally, it seems a sure rule that anyone who fulminates against coffee is either a bore or a fraud, if not both. A young woman walks past me in the wine area, interrupting my foodist reverie as she explains to her friend in sympathetic tones: 'Joe and Massie are having a sit-down.' Frankly, I don't blame them. I go home and cook a big fry-up.

On one 2011 episode of *MasterChef: The Professionals*, the voiceover explains reverently: 'This is fine dining now, so Steve must remove the outer skin from each individual pea.'[4] Were they not so hilariously serious, one might take it as an excellent joke on the fetishization of pointless labour that characterizes so much modern foodism. (As Angela Carter wrote of Alice Waters's quest for the perfect melon: 'This rapt, bug-eyed concern with the small print not even of life but of gluttony is, I think, genuinely decadent.')[5] But even for the unfine dining that most of us actually practise, the cultural pressure to devote more of our mental energy to food has an unsavoury insistence about it. The amiable modern 'food adventurer' Stefan Gates, who performs live food shows where he creates 'carrot instruments' and demonstrates 'custard-powder flamethrowing', and exults in serving people lamb's testicles ('I live up in north London and there's a brilliant Turkish butcher's, and he was a little bit surprised when I asked for twenty-seven kilos of testicles'), explains that his ambition is to make people 'think' about food.[6] Potential concern for ethical issues aside, why exactly *should* we think more about food than many of us already do? Why is thinking more about food a good thing per se, rather than thinking more about unemployment, or metaphysics, or heavy metal? Joanna Blythman cites it as an appalling statistic that, in Britain, 38 per cent of women and 57 per cent of men 'have little interest in food',[7] as though they are zombies, for all that they might have profound interests in art history or engineering. By their blithe example such people threaten to shame the crazed foodist, who must therefore in *ressentiment* rain down moralistic imprecations on these brutish gobblers for whom eating is not the very point of existence. Becoming interested in food is itself now an ethical obligation.

One alarming possible reason why is offered by the report of a 2011 'study' sponsored by Président, the cheese and butter company, according to which British people spent an average total of thirty-nine minutes eating per day. For some people who are more interested in other things, this is no doubt an index of the wonderful efficiency of modern civilization, compared to how much time their ancestors had to waste in the getting and preparing of food. For others to whom such attenuated eating time represents, equally reasonably, a loss of conviviality, the problem is not one of attitude but one of time. But the tabloid-newspaper report or massaged press release on this 'study' was revealingly incoherent on the matter. Britons spent so little time eating because they were 'under so much pressure at home and at work', but the answer to their woes, supplied by 'psychologist Dr Richard Woolfson, from Président', was simply to ignore that pressure and sacrifice whatever else was needed to devoting more hours to eating. 'Our study shows Britons are not taking the time to properly enjoy their meals,' Woolfson lamented. 'It is so important to take the time to taste and appreciate food, as this has an effect on our emotional and physical well-being and can affect our productivity.'[8]

Ah, our *productivity*. And so, to add to the 'pressure' of normal work and family life, the psychologist with the cheese patron piles guilt on top, if you fail to obey what Slavoj Žižek calls the superego injunction to enjoy: not only must you eat food, you must enjoy it in the right way. Your 'free time' (which, as Guy Debord noted, is that time given back to you after the 'violent expropriation' of most of it)[9] is not actually 'free' after all, because you are obliged to spend it in the enjoyment of eating. That will make you happier, the cheese-psychologist promises; but, more important, it will make you more *productive*. (Fitter, happier . . .) In other words, you must want to enjoy refuelling yourself so that you can labour more efficiently when you go to work the next day. (Foodism is the opiate of the people.) And so much the better if, at the times when one is not either working or eating with the correct amount of enjoyment, one gazes at displays of virtual eating on the television in the evening, and at the weekend makes a pilgrimage to MasterChef Live in order to witness even more virtual eating in the starry flesh, as well as haunting the stands so as to plan rationally how, in the future, one can enjoy one's eating even more, thus soaring ever upwards on the glorious productivity escalator, able to plough the profits back into yet greater investments in preparation time and local artisan produce, achieving some day the ideally blissful psychic state in which thoughts of eating and working fill and perfect all one's waking hours, till one has at last eaten one's fill of time on Earth.

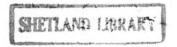

'At the end of the day, it's just food, isn't it? Just food.'
Marco Pierre White, *White Heat*

Acknowledgements

The author wishes to thank Alex Clark, Rosalind Porter, Lesley Levene, Maugan Lloyd, Kari Lloyd, Anna Richards, Tam Murray-Threipland, Daniel Fugallo, Schuyler W. Henderson, Lucien Jones, Sarah Lefevre, Pascal Wyse, Charlie English, Justine Cottle, Jonny Hill, Kristy MacDonald, and Emelie Henriksson. Thanks also to the staff of the British Library.

Bibliophagy

Adorno, Theodor, *Negative Dialectics* (1966; New York, 2005)

Adorno, Theodor, and Horkheimer, Max, *Towards a New Manifesto* (London, 2011)

Allan, Tony, *Virtual Water* (London, 2011)

Anon. ('G.V.'), *Dinners and Dinner-Parties* (London, 1862)

Aquinas, Thomas, *On Evil*, ed. Richard J. Regan and Brian Davies (Oxford, 2003)

Barr, Ann, and Levy, Paul, *The Official Foodie Handbook* (London, 1984)

Barthes, Roland, 'Towards a Psychosociology of Contemporary Food Consumption' (1961), in Carole Counihan and Penny Van Esterik, (eds.) *Food and Culture: A Reader* (1997; New York, 2008), 28–35

Blackwood, Caroline, and Haycraft, Anna, *Darling, You Shouldn't Have Gone to So Much Trouble* (London, 1980)

Blumenthal, Heston, *The Fat Duck Cookbook* (2008; London, 2009)

—, *Heston's Fantastical Feasts* (London, 2010)

—, *Heston Blumenthal at Home* (London, 2011)

Blythman, Joanna, *Bad Food Britain* (London, 2006)

Boulestin, X.M., *Myself, My Two Countries . . .* (London, 1936)

Bourdain, Anthony, *Kitchen Confidential* (2000; London, 2004)

—, *A Cook's Tour* (2001; London, 2004)

173

—, *Medium Raw* (London, 2010)

Brillat-Savarin, Jean Anthelme, *The Pleasures of the Table* (London, 2011)

Buchanan, Allen, *Better Than Human* (Oxford, 2011)

Burton, Robert, *The Anatomy of Melancholy* (1621; Glasgow, 1824).

Child, Julia, *My Life in France* (2006; London, 2009)

Clapp, Jennifer, *Food* (London, 2011)

Dahl, Sophie, *Miss Dahl's Voluptuous Delights* (London, 2009)

David, Elizabeth, *A Book of Mediterranean Food* (1950; London, 1958)

Debord, Guy, *Society of the Spectacle*, trans. Donald Nicholson-Smith (1967; New York, 1994)

Deighton, Len, *Action Cook Book* (London, 1965)

Derrida, Jacques, 'Il faut bien manger; ou, Le calcul du sujet', in Derrida, Jacques, ed. Weber, Elisabeth, *Points de suspension: Entretiens* (Paris, 1992), 269-301.

Douglas, Norman, *Venus in the Kitchen* (1952; London, 1971)

Driver, Christopher, *The British at Table 1940–1980* (London, 1983)

Ehrlich, Max, *The Edict* (London, 1972)

Escoffier, A., *A Guide to Modern Cookery* (London, 1907)

Fearnley-Whittingstall, Hugh, *A Cook on the Wild Side* (London, 1997)

Foer, Jonathan Safran, *Eating Animals* (London, 2009)

Gilbert, Elizabeth, *Eat, Pray, Love* (London, 2006)

Goldacre, Ben, *Bad Science* (London, 2008)

Goody, Jack, *Cooking, Cuisine, and Class* (Cambridge, 1982)

Gottlieb, Julie V., and Linehan, Thomas P., *The Culture of Fascism: Visions of the Far Right in Britain* (London, 2004)

Henderson, Fergus, *Nose to Tail Eating: A Kind of British Cooking* (London, 1999)

Holford, Patrick, *The Optimum Nutrition Bible* (1997; London, 1998)

—, *Patrick Holford's New Optimum Nutrition Bible* (London, 2004)

Johnston, Josée, and Baumann, Shyon, *Foodies: Democracy and Distinction in the Gourmet Foodscape* (New York, 2010)

Jones, Lucien, *The Transparent Head* (Cambridge, 2006)

Kalaga, Wojciech H., and Rachwal, Tadeusz (eds.), *Feeding Culture* (Frankfurt, 2005)

Kass, Leon R., *The Hungry Soul: Eating and the Perfecting of Our Nature* (1994; Chicago, 1999)

Keller, Thomas, *The French Laundry Cookbook* (New York, 1999)

—, *Ad Hoc at Home* (New York, 2009)

Lamb, Charles, *A Dissertation on Roast Pig and Other Essays* (London, 2011)

Lappé, Frances Moore, *Diet for a Small Planet* (1971; New York, 1974)

Levenstein, Harvey, *Paradox of Plenty: A Social History of Eating in America* (1993; Oxford, 1994)

Lewis, C.S., *Mere Christianity* (1952; London, 2001)

Linford, Jenny, *Writing About Food* (London, 1996)

Livy, *History of Rome*, ed. Rev. Canon Roberts (New York, 1912); Perseus online edn.

McGee, Harold, *McGee on Food and Cooking* (London, 2004)

McKeith, Gillian, *Gillian McKeith's Food Bible* (London, 2008)

Marinetti, Filippo Tommaso, *The Futurist Cookbook*, trans. Suzanne Brill (San Francisco, 1989)

McWilliams, James E., *Just Food* (New York, 2009)

Newnham-Davis, Lieut.-Col., *Dinners and Diners: Where and How to Dine in London* (London, 1899)

Northbourne, Lord, *Look to the Land* (London, 1940)

Oliver, Jamie, *Jamie's Kitchen* (London, 2002)

—, *Jamie's Great Britain* (London, 2011)

Oxford English Dictionary, 3rd edn (2008); online version, September 2011

Paltrow, Gwyneth, *Notes from My Kitchen* (London, 2011)

Pennell, Elizabeth Robins, *The Feasts of Autolycus: The Diary of a Greedy Woman* (1896; London, 2003)

Pigott, Sudi, *How to Be a Better Foodie* (2006; London, 2008)

Plato, *Republic*, trans. Paul Shorey, in *Plato in Twelve Volumes*, Vols. 5 and 6 (Cambridge, MA, 1969); Perseus online edn.

Pollan, Michael, *The Omnivore's Dilemma* (2006; London, 2007)

—, *In Defence of Food* (London, 2008)

Poole, Steven, *Unspeak* (London, 2006)

Prose, Francine, *Gluttony* (Oxford, 2003)

Raimbault, A.T., *Le Parfait Cuisinier, ou, Le Breviaire des Gourmands* (Paris, 1811)

Reichl, Ruth, *Garlic and Sapphires* (2005; London, 2006)

Robbe-Grillet, Alain, *Why I Love Barthes* (London, 2011)

Rombauer, Irma S., *The Joy of Cooking* (1931; New York, 1936)

Scapp, Ron, and Seitz, Brian (eds.), *Eating Culture* (New York, 1998)

Scruton, Roger, *I Drink Therefore I Am* (2009; London, 2010)

Sen, Amartya, *The Idea of Justice* (London, 2009)

Sinclair, Upton, *The Jungle* (1906; Harmondsworth, 1965)

Singer, Peter, and Mason, Jim, *Eating: What We Eat and Why It Matters* (London, 2006)

Slater, Nigel, *Toast* (2003; London, 2004)

Smith, Alisa, and MacKinnon, J.B., *Plenty* (New York, 2007)

Smith, Delia, *How to Cheat at Cooking* (1971; London, 1973)

Smith, Gilly, *The Jamie Oliver Effect: The Man, The Food, The Revolution* (2006; London, 2008)

Soyer, Alexis, *The Chef at War* (London, 2011)

Steingarten, Jeffrey, *The Man Who Ate Everything* (New York, 1997)

Stelzer, Cita, *Dinner with Churchill* (London, 2011)

This, Hervé, *The Science of the Oven* (New York, 2009a)

—, *Building a Meal* (New York, 2009b)

Visser, Margaret, *The Rituals of Dinner* (Toronto, 1991)

White, Marco Pierre, *White Heat* (London, 1990)

Zola, Emile, *The Belly of Paris*, trans. Brian Nelson (Oxford, 2007)

Notes

Prologue: The Food Rave

1. 'Alex James: Cheese Saved My Life', *Mirror*, 28 July 2009.
2. *Jamie's Great Britain*, Episode 1, Channel 4, 25 October 2011.
3. Nigella Lawson, 'My Love Affair with Salted Caramel', *Stylist*, 7 December 2011.

1. You Aren't What You Eat

1. Matt Rudd, 'The Trouble with Being Jamie', *Sunday Times*, 25 September 2011.
2. Linford, 52–3.
3. Chaniga Vorasarun, 'Ten Top-Earning Celebrity Chefs', forbes.com, 8 August 2008.
4. Ann Lee, 'Gordon Ramsay Film Debut Love's Kitchen is £121 Flop at the Box Office', *Metro*, 30 June 2011.
5. Tom Mitchelson, 'The Mousse Hunter', *The Times*, 6 October 2011.
6. Allan Jenkins, 'El Bulli: The Ultimate Dining Experience', *Observer*, 19 June 2011.
7. Barr and Levy, 7.
8. www.food.unt.edu.
9. Frank Bruni, 'Dinner and Derangement', *New York Times*, 18 October 2011.

10. Barr and Levy, 25.
11. *OED*, 'foodie' n.; Gael Greene, 'What's Nouvelle? La Cuisine Bourgeoise', *New York* magazine, 2 June 1980.
12. *OED*, 'foodist' n.
13. Steven Bratman, 'The Health Food Eating Disorder', *Yoga Journal*, October 1997.
14. Owen Gibson, 'TV Dietician to Stop Using Title Dr in Adverts', *Guardian*, 12 February 2007.
15. McKeith, 22.
16. Ibid., 147.
17. Ibid., 188.
18. Ibid., 199.
19. Pollan (2008), 1.
20. McKeith, 244.
21. Ibid., 18.
22. Ibid., 174.
23. A. Fasano et al., 'Prevalence of Celiac Disease in at-Risk and Not-at-Risk Groups in the United States: A Large Multicenter Study', *Archives of Internal Medicine*, Vol. 163, No. 3 (10 February 2003), 286–92; Keith O'Brien, 'Should We All Go Gluten-Free?', *New York Times*, 25 November 2011.
24. House of Lords, 'Science and Technology – Sixth Report', 24 July 2007, 8.40.
25. Burton, 36.
26. Chloë Taylor, 'Foucault and the Ethics of Eating', *Foucault Studies*, No. 9 (September 2010), 72.
27. Jon Henley, 'Britain's Food Habits: How Well Do We Eat?', *Guardian*, 10 May 2011.
28. McKeith, 6.
29. Goldacre, 132.
30. Holford (1997), ix.
31. Ibid., 155.

32. Holford (1997), 79; patrickholford.com
33. Holford (2004), 173, 208, 460, 357.
34. Holford (1997), 168–74; Holford (2004), 275–87.
35. Holford (2004), 1.
36. Patrick Holford, 'Letter: My Right to be Called a Nutritionist', *Guardian*, 16 February 2007.
37. L.M. Donini et al., 'Orthorexia Nervosa: A Preliminary Study with a Proposal for Diagnosis and an Attempt to Measure the Dimension of the Phenomenon', *Eating Weight Discord*, Vol. 9, No. 2 (2004), 154–5.
38. Brillat-Savarin, 1.
39. Ibid.
40. Ibid., 54.
41. Jay Rayner, 'Greed isn't Bad. But Epic Meal Time's Gluttony is Just Too Much', *Observer*, 11 December 2011.
42. Barthes, 33.
43. Lamb, 17.
44. Sen, 342.
45. Phil Izzo, 'Some 15% of U.S. Uses Food Stamps', *Wall Street Journal*, 1 November 2011.
46. Sean Michaels, 'Jon Bon Jovi Opens "Pay What You Can" Restaurant', *Guardian*, 20 October 2011.
47. John Prescott, interviewed on 'Future Food', *The Food Programme*, BBC Radio 4, 13 November 2011.
48. Adorno, 23.
49. Angela Carter, 'Noovs' Hoovs in the Trough', *London Review of Books*, 24 January 1985.

2. Soul Food

1. Pollan (2008), 6.
2. Pollan (2006), 9, 411.
3. Fearnley-Whittingstall, 167.

4. Prose, 38–9.

5. Henry John Todd (ed.), *The Works of Edmund Spenser* (London, 1805), Vol. II, 125 (*The Faerie Queene*, Book I, Canto IV, XIII).

6. Aquinas, 412.

7. B.R. Myers, 'The Moral Crusade Against Foodies', *Atlantic*, March 2011.

8. Bourdain (2000), 261.

9. Chloë Taylor, 'Foucault and the Ethics of Eating', *Foucault Studies*, No. 9 (September 2010), 77.

10. Denis Campbell, 'How to Save School Dinners – Part Two', *Guardian*, 24 October 2011.

11. Jamie Oliver, 'This Obesity Strategy is a Cop-out', *Guardian*, 13 October 2011.

12. Giles Tremlett, 'Chefs Aim to Save the World', *Guardian*, 12 September 2011.

13. Blumenthal (2008), 126.

14. Keller (1999), 209.

15. *Historia Augusta*, Commodus 11.1, at penelope.uchicago.edu/ Thayer/E/Roman/Texts/Historia_Augusta/Commodus*.html.

16. Rombauer, Foreword.

17. Sharon Hendry, 'I Just Want to Cook a Good Roast', *Sun*, 18 September 2010.

18. John Crace, 'Maya Angelou: "I Make No Apologies for Writing a Cookbook"', *Guardian*, 2 November 2011.

3. The Hunger Artists

1. Julia Pine, 'Breaking Dalinian Bread: On Consuming the Anthropomorphic, Performative, Ferocious, and Eucharistic Loaves of Salvador Dalí', *Invisible Culture*, Vol. 14 (2010).

2. Barr and Levy, 6.

3. Steingarten, 384.

4. Bourdain (2000), 270.

5. 'Future Food', *The Food Programme*, BBC Radio 4, 13 November 2011.

6. Joanna Moorhead, 'From El Bulli to the Family Kitchen', *Guardian*, 1 October 2011.

7. 'The Week in Books', *Guardian*, 25 June 2011.

8. Blumenthal (2008), 424.

9. *Q*, January 2012, 104.

10. Keller (1999), 292.

11. This (2009b), 99.

12. Driver, 130–31.

13. Helen Lewis Hasteley, 'If Music Can Be Art, Why Can't Food?', *New Statesman*, 5 July 2011.

14. 'Future Food', *The Food Programme*, BBC Radio 4, 13 November 2011.

15. John Lanchester, 'The Mad Genius of "Modernist Cuisine"', *New Yorker*, 21 March 2011.

16. Blumenthal (2010), 21.

17. 'Rolling Stones "Let It Bleed" Original Artwork with Delia Smith Cake on up for Sale', mirror.co.uk, 22 November 2011.

18. Lanchester, 'The Mad Genius of "Modernist Cuisine"', *New Yorker*, 21 March 2011.

19. Soyer, 32.

20. *Heston's Mission Impossible*, Episode 4, Channel 4, 15 March 2011.

21. Soyer, 97.

22. Escoffier, vii.

23. Bourdain (2001), 7.

24. Blumenthal (2008), 127.

25. Ibid., 107.

26. Ibid., 211.

27. Livy, Book 39, 9.

28. Plato, 2.372b–e.

29. Marinetti, 172.

30. Ibid., 40.
31. Livy, Book 39, 8.
32. Marinetti, 39.
33. Marinetti, 40; Blumenthal (2008), 137, 148; Jones, 42.
34. Florence Fabricant, 'The Future Arrives on Park Avenue', *New York Times*, 23 February 2009.
35. 'Future Food', *The Food Programme*, BBC Radio 4, 13 November 2011.
36. Marinetti, 33, 97.

4. Word Soup

1. Robbe-Grillet, 69.
2. Barthes, 31.
3. Yeomans and Chambers, 'Effects of Flavour Expectation on Liking: From Pleasure to Disgust', in Blumenthal (2008), 503.
4. Slavoj Žižek, 'Psychoanalysis in Post-Marxism: The Case of Alain Badiou', *South Atlantic Quarterly*, Spring 1998.
5. 'L'Enclume', *The Trip*, Episode 2, BBC Two, 8 November 2010.
6. Pigott, 231.
7. Ellen Jackson, 'Spring Lamb', *Edible Portland*, Spring 2008.
8. Ibid.
9. Blumenthal (2008), 137.
10. This (2009a), 165.
11. Ibid., 175.
12. Johnston and Baumann, 26; www.alinea-restaurant.com.
13. The Spiteful Chef, 'My Threesome with Chef Achatz', 15 April 2009, thespitefulchef.blogspot.com.
14. Reichl, 217.
15. David A. Fahrenthold, 'Unpopular, Unfamiliar Fish Species Suffer from Becoming Seafood', *Washington Post*, 31 July 2009.
16. Zerrin, 'A Food Name Change', GiveRecipe.com, 18 September 2011.

17. *Jamie's Great Britain*, Episode 1, Channel 4, 25 October 2011.
18. jamieoliver.com.
19. White, 115.

5. Sex on a Plate

1. B.R. Myers, 'The Moral Crusade Against Foodies', *Atlantic*, March 2011.
2. Gilbert, 286–7.
3. Bourdain (2010), 198–202.
4. Jay Rayner, 'Oyster, Figs – Does Any Food Really Work as an Aphrodisiac?', *Observer*, 18 September 2011.
5. Slater, 244.
6. Cited in David Farrell Krell, 'Eating Out: Voluptuosity for Dessert', in Scapp and Seitz, 78.
7. Barr and Levy, 20.
8. Susan Bell, 'France's Songbird Delicacy is Outlawed', *Telegraph*, 9 September 2007.
9. Bourdain (2010), xv.
10. Deborah R. Geis, 'Feeding the Audience: Food, Feminism, and Performance Art', in Scapp and Seitz, 221.
11. John Walsh, 'Chez Bruce', *Independent*, 3 September 2011.
12. Cited in Linford, 36.
13. Newnham-Davis, 43.
14. Oliver (2002), 99.
15. White, 56.
16. Alexander Cockburn, 'Gastro-Porn', *New York Review of Books*, 8 December 1977.
17. Ehrlich, 172–3.
18. Linford, 13.
19. Barr and Levy, 103.
20. Ibid.
21. Paltrow, 189.

22. Bourdain (2010), 84.

23. Ibid., 90–91.

24. Zola, 34–5.

25. Jay Rayner, 'Greed isn't Bad. But Epic Meal Time's Gluttony is Just Too Much', *Observer*, 11 December 2011.

26. Douglas, 126.

27. Raimbault, 92.

28. Ibid., 83.

29. Heston Blumenthal, 'Do Yourself a Flavour Favour: Try a Bee Omelette', *Times*, 6 October 2011.

30. Alice Weinreb, 'Taste No Evil: The Dangers of the Mouth in Ancient Rome', in Kalaga and Rachwal, 169.

31. Ibid., 171.

32. Plato, 8.559b–e.

33. Bourdain (2001), 187.

6. Fashion on a Fork

1. Goody, 152.

2. Anon. ('G.V.'), 56.

3. Blumenthal (2008), 26.

4. Escoffier, 260.

5. Barr and Levy, 7.

6. Blumenthal (2008), 130.

7. Steingarten, 180.

8. Linford, 35.

9. Ibid., 11.

10. Pigott, 137.

11. Rachel Cooke, 'Why Pheasant is the Only Game in Town', *Observer*, 18 September 2011.

12. Vanessa Thorpe, 'Apps Become the Secret Ingredient in the Battle of the Celebrity Christmas Cookbooks', *Guardian*, 13 November 2011.

13. 'Food Fashions: Five Decades of Food Fads', *At Home Taste with Marco Pierre White*, October 2011.

14. 'Gastropub RIP . . .', goodfoodguide.co.uk, 4 September 2011.

15. This (2009a), 4.

16. This (2009b), 109.

17. This (2009a), 176.

18. 'Hipping Hall', *The Trip*, Episode 4, BBC Two, 22 November 2010.

19. twitter.com/suzanne_moore/status/146705329403609088.

20. Frank Bruni, 'Dinner and Derangement', *New York Times*, 17 October 2011.

21. White, 108.

22. Anon ('G.V.'), 7.

23. Driver, 183.

24. Johnston and Baumann, xv.

25. John G. Watters, 'The Manners of Mass Murder: Eating Fear', in Kalaga and Rachwal, 95–6.

26. Martin Caraher, 'Bad Behaviour in the Kitchen: Blaming the Cook Not the Perpetrator!', Wellcome Trust seminar, 29 September 2011.

27. Sheena S. Iyengar and Mark R. Lepper, 'When Choice is Demotivating: Can One Desire Too Much of a Good Thing?', *Journal of Personality and Social Psychology*, Vol. 79, No. 6, 2000, 995–1006.

7. Consuming History

1. Tracy MacLeod, 'Dinner by Heston Blumenthal', *Independent*, 12 February 2011.

2. Barthes, 32.

3. Lauren Collins, 'The King's Meal', *New Yorker*, 21 November 2011, 69.

4. Ibid., 68.

5. Ibid., 71.

6. 'McDonald's Prepares 1955 Burger for UK Debut', burgerbusiness. com, 25 August 2011.

7. A.A. Gill, 'Table Talk: Cut at 45 Park Lane', *Sunday Times*, 25 September 2011.

8. Paul Theroux, 'Heirlooms', *New Yorker*, 21 November 2011, 72.

9. *Jamie's Great Britain*, Episode I, Channel 4, 25 October 2011.

10. Alan Travis, 'Pickles to Serve up Curry College in Government Integration Strategy', *Guardian*, 18 November 2011.

11. Jamie Oliver, 'Make Me Happy' (extract from *Jamie's Great Britain*), *Sunday Times*, 25 September 2011.

12. Ibid.

13. David Sexton, 'Are You Ready for Another Helping of Jamie Oliver?', *London Evening Standard*, 17 October 2011.

14. Collins, 'The King's Meal', *New Yorker*, 21 November 2011, 71.

8. The Real Thing

1. Child, 191.

2. Ibid., 254.

3. Alison Tyler, 'Everyone Back to Mine: Pop-up Restaurants in Private Homes are the Latest Foodie Fad', *Independent*, 4 June 2009.

4. Liz Hoggard, 'All Aboard the Number 30', *London Evening Standard*, 6 October 2011.

5. Nick Wyke, 'Take Me to the French!', *The Times*, 6 October 2011.

6. Ibid.

7. Lizzie Collingham, 'Chequered History of an Ideal Food', *Times Literary Supplement*, 7 October 2011, 31.

8. David, 79.

9. Dahl, 146.

10. Henderson, 57.

11. Keller (1999), 47

12. Ibid., 73.

13. Ibid., 156.

14. Blythman, 124.

15. Bourdain (2010), 108.

16. David Sexton, '"Chav" Ramsay Will Give Jamie and Nando's a Run for Their Money', *London Evening Standard*, 27 September 2011.

17. Mina Holland, 'Gourmet Salt: Seasoned Cooks Know Its Place', guardian.co.uk, 18 November 2011.

18. Levenstein, 140.

19. David Sexton, 'Are You Ready for Another Helping of Jamie Oliver?', *London Evening Standard*, 17 October 2011.

20. Goody, 99–100.

21. Ibid., 103, 115, 130.

22. Blythman, 126.

23. Cited in Driver, 16.

24. Jon Henley, 'Britain's Food Habits: How Well Do We Eat?', *Guardian*, 10 May 2011.

25. 'Future Food', *The Food Programme*, BBC Radio 4, 13 November 2011.

26. Barthes, 30.

27. Blythman, 51.

28. Julie Andrieu, *Le B.A.-ba du chocolat* (Paris, 2011).

29. Helen Pidd and Lars Eriksen, 'Swedish Chef Leila Lindholm's Butter Fingers "Causing National Shortage"', *Guardian*, 23 September 2011.

30. David Dubois et al., 'Super Size Me: Product Size as a Signal of Status', *Journal of Consumer Research*, Vol. 38, April 2012.

31. Frank Bruni, 'Unsavory Culinary Elitism', *New York Times*, 24 August 2011.

9. Back to Nature

1. A.A. Gill, 'Table Talk', *Sunday Times*, 25 September 2011.

2. Keller (1999), 2.

3. Bourdain (2004), 245.

4. Ibid., 191.

5. Henderson, vii.

6. Ibid., 114, 143.

7. Pollan (2008), 200.

8. Scruton, 33; Pigott, 230.

9. *OED, terroir* n.

10. This (2009a), 65–6.

11. Gilly Smith, 226.

12. Brendan O'Neill, 'Is Junk Food a Myth?', BBC News, 3 October 2005.

13. 'Food for Thought: Obesity and Addiction', *Brain Briefings*, Society for Neuroscience, January 2012.

14. Levenstein, 16.

15. This (2009b), 38.

16. Goody, 169–73.

17. Levenstein, 202.

18. Gottlieb and Linehan, 188.

19. John Paull, 'The Farm as Organism: The Foundational Idea of Organic Agriculture', *Elementals: Journal of Bio-Dynamics Tasmania*, No. 83 (2006), 14–18.

20. McGee, 3.

21. Rob Johnston, 'The Great Organic Myths: Why Organic Foods are an Indulgence the World Can't Afford', *Independent*, 1 May 2008.

22. Peter Melchett, 'The Great Organic Myths Rebutted', *Independent*, 8 May 2008.

23. Buchanan, 51.

24. John Vidal, 'Bolivia Enshrines Natural World's Rights with Equal Status for Mother Earth', *Guardian*, 10 April 2011.

25. This (2009b), 105, 79.

26. www.food.gov.uk/foodindustry/farmingfood/organicfood/; 'Ad Watchdog Raps Organic Claims', BBC News, 3 March 2005.

27. McWilliams, 216.

28. Clapp, 55.
29. McWilliams, 109.
30. Johnston and Baumann, 28.
31. Rebecca Smithers, 'Organic Food and Drink Sales Slump', *Guardian*, 15 December 2011.
32. Greg Easterbrook, 'Forgotten Benefactor of Humanity', *Atlantic*, January 1997.
33. McWilliams, 115.
34. Levenstein, 199.
35. Bourdain (2010), 131–2.
36. Sinclair, 406.
37. Ibid., 407–8.
38. Cited in Levenstein, 142.

10. Eating to Utopia

1. Pollan (2006), 258.
2. Johnston and Baumann, 138.
3. Cited in B.R. Myers, 'The Moral Crusade Against Foodies', *Atlantic*, March 2011.
4. Johnston and Bauman, 142.
5. Alexandra Topping, 'René Redzepi's Noma Tops List of World's Best Restaurants', *Guardian*, 27 April 2010.
6. Blumenthal (2008), 10.
7. Smith and MacKinnon, back-jacket blurb.
8. Singer and Mason, 156.
9. Pollan (2006), 245.
10. McWilliams, 48.
11. Allan, ix ff.
12. Tara Garnett, 'Cooking up a Storm: Food, Greenhouse Gas Emissions and Our Changing Climate', Food Climate Research Network, September 2008.
13. Singer and Mason, 146.

14. McWilliams, 24–6.

15. Pollan (2006), 256.

16. McWilliams, 30.

17. Clapp, 31.

18. Stephanie Lacava, 'It Takes a Village', *New York Times* Style Magazine, 1 November 2011.

19. Johnston and Baumann, 170.

20. Lappé, xiv, 3.

21. Clapp, 177.

22. Lisa Cassidy, 'Women Shopping/Women Sweatshopping', in Jessica Wolfendale and Jeanette Kennett (eds.), *Fashion – Philosophy for Everyone* (London, 2011), 193–4.

23. 'Future Food', *The Food Programme*, BBC Radio 4, 13 November 2011.

24. Darra Goldstein, 'Going to Extremes', *Gastronomica*, Vol. 11, No. 3, Fall 2011.

25. Victoria Barret, 'Dropbox: The Inside Story of Tech's Hottest Startup', *Forbes*, 18 October 2011.

26. Jane Kramer, 'The Food at Our Feet', *New Yorker*, 21 November 2011, 80.

27. Ibid., 82.

28. Ibid., 84–5.

29. *OED*, forage *v.*

30. Kramer, 'The Food at Our Feet', *New Yorker*, 21 November 2011, 87.

31. Ibid., 88.

32. Ibid., 90.

33. Katharine Hibbert, 'I Eat out of Bins Too. So What?', guardian.co.uk, 15 February 2011.

11. The Great Escape

1. Cited in Blackwood and Haycraft, 211.

2. Blumenthal (2010), 21.

3. www.unilever.co.uk/brands/foodbrands/Pot_Noodle.aspx.

4. Victoria Stewart, 'Down the Cakehole: Health Pots', *London Evening Standard*, 6 October 2011.

5. 'Preview: Next's Childhood Menu', *Metromix Chicago*, 18 October 2011; Ari Bendersky, 'Next Restaurant's Childhood Menu in Photos and Video', *Eater Chicago*, 24 October 2011.

6. David, ix.

7. Driver, 12.

8. Johnston and Baumann, 163.

9. Cited in Goody, 104.

10. Cited in David, 49.

11. Richard Godwin, 'How Food Has Become Our Security', *London Evening Standard*, 12 October 2011.

12. Levenstein, 248–9.

13. Blumenthal (2011), 389.

14. Jonathan Prynn, 'It's El Bulli for You as Best Chef in the World Publishes a Family Cookbook', *London Evening Standard*, 29 September 2011.

15. Keller (2009), 1.

16. Ibid., 125.

17. White, 8.

12. Time, Gentlemen, Please

1. Keller (1999), 2.

2. Driver, ix.

3. Pollan (2008), 194–5.

4. Yasmin Alibhai-Brown, cited in Blythman, 12.

5. Michael Pollan, 'The 36-Hour Dinner Party', *New York Times Magazine*, 10 October 2010.

6. Blythman, 96.

7. Barthes, 32.

8. Gilly Smith, 183.

9. Blythman, xv.

10. Pollan (2008), 148.
11. Johnston and Baumann, 25.
12. Adorno and Horkheimer, 32.
13. Anon. ('G.V.'), I, 5–6.
14. Pennell, 3.
15. Driver, 98.
16. Delia Smith, 2.
17. Ibid., 81.
18. Ibid., 114.
19. Jon Henley, 'First, Take Your Frozen Mash . . .', *Guardian*, 14 March 2008.
20. Blackwood and Haycraft, 9, 16, 36.
21. Ibid., 37.
22. Cited in Gilly Smith, 225–6.
23. Boulestin, 131.
24. Deighton, 136.
25. John Walsh, 'A Taste of the Action: Len Deighton's Cult Sixties Cookbook is Back', *Independent*, 18 June 2009.
26. Blythman, 8.
27. White, 11.
28. Blumenthal (2008), 29.
29. Bourdain (2000), 57.
30. Poole, 238; Foer, 33.
31. Steingarten, 428–9.
32. This (2009a), 12.
33. Bourdain (2010), 203.
34. Gilbert, 64

13. Il Faut Bien Manger

1. Delia Smith, 23.
2. Kass, 5–7.
3. Ibid., 170, 186, 173.

4. Derrida, 296–7.

5. Scruton, 144, 162.

6. Visser, 262.

7. This (2009a), 165.

8. Alain de Botton, 'Alain de Botton's Perfect Dinner Party', *The Times*, 27 May 2010.

9. guardian.co.uk/discussion/comment-permalink/5683317.

10. Jane Kramer, 'The Food at Our Feet', *New Yorker*, 21 November 2011, 90.

11. Thanks to Padgett Powell.

12. Barthes, 33.

13. Jamie Oliver, 'Make Me Happy', *Sunday Times*, 25 September 2011.

14. Johnston and Baumann, 61.

14. Envoi: Virtual Eating

1. Henry Barnes, 'Franc Roddam: From Parkas to the Perfect Soufflé', *Guardian*, 9 November 2011.

2. Lewis, 96 (thanks to Rebecca Lambert-Smith).

3. Keller (2009), 226.

4. Cited in 'Pseuds Corner', *Private Eye*, No. 1305, 13 January 2012, 30.

5. Angela Carter, 'Noovs' Hoovs in the Trough', *London Review of Books*, 24 January 1985.

6. 'Future Food', *The Food Programme*, BBC Radio 4, 13 November 2011.

7. Blythman, xv.

8. 'The 39-minute Meals', *Daily Mail*, 25 July 2011.

9. Debord, 159.

Index